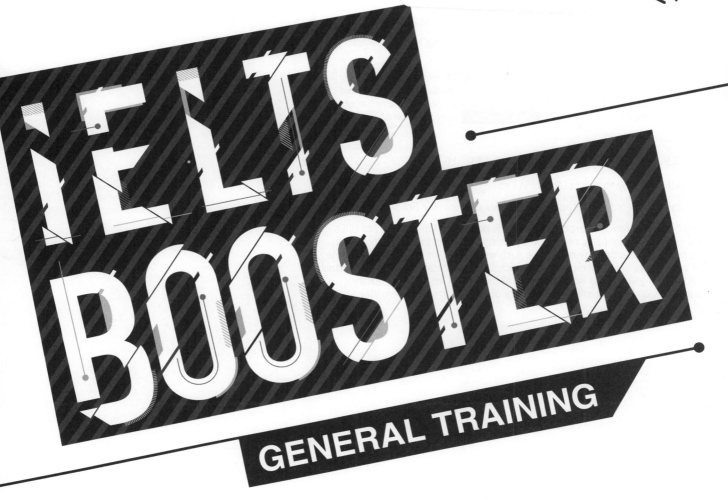

IELTS BOOSTER

GENERAL TRAINING

Photocopiable exam resources for teachers

WITH AUDIO

Deborah Hobbs and Susan Hutchison

Cambridge University Press and Assessment
www.cambridge.org/elt

Cambridge Assessment English
www.cambridgeenglish.org

Information on this title: www.cambridge.org/9781009249058

First published 2022

20 19 18 17 16 15 14 13 12 11 10 9 8 7 6 5 4 3 2 1

Printed in India by Multivista Global Pvt Ltd.

A catalogue record for this publication is available from the British Library

CONTENTS

MAP OF THE BOOK

Listening	Topic and question type
Worksheet 1 Pages 12–15	**Dolphins** Avoiding word matching Paraphrasing Multiple-choice questions
Worksheet 2 Pages 16–19	**Studying and work** Paraphrasing Signposting Contradiction Matching questions
Worksheet 3 Pages 20–23	**Films and filmmaking** Signposting language Process Sentence completion
Worksheet 4 Pages 24–28	**Maps** Map labelling Understand and follow directions Sentence completion Compass icon
Worksheet 5 Pages 29–31	**Animals in the wild** Similarities Using singular or plural nouns Noticing errors Table completion
Worksheet 6 Pages 32–34	**Design competition** Note completion Synonyms and paraphrases Predicting word types Sentence completion

Reading	Topic and question type
Worksheet 1 Pages 35–38	**Juicers** Paraphrasing Matching statements
Worksheet 2 Pages 39–41	**Tiritiri Matangi Island Day Trip – New Zealand** Key words True/False/Not given statements
Worksheet 3 Pages 42–45	**Working as a greenkeeper – Western Australia** Sentence completion Paraphrasing
Worksheet 4 Pages 46–49	**The mystery of the incredible human brain** Answering questions Question words and key words

Writing

	Topic and task type
Worksheet 1 **Pages 50–54**	**Letter of complaint** Style and tone Formal letter Identifying the task
Worksheet 2 **Pages 55–59**	**Job application** Answering all points in the task Suitable phrases Proofreading
Worksheet 3 **Pages 60–63**	**A personal letter** Functional language Writing an informal letter Identifying the task
Worksheet 4 **Pages 64–69**	**Discussion essay** Presenting an argument Supporting a point Following a plan Writing an introduction and a conclusion
Worksheet 5 **Pages 70–76**	**Double question essay** Agreeing or disagreeing Linking words

Speaking

	Topic and task type
Worksheet 1 **Pages 77–80**	**Friends and family** Speaking Part 1 Words and phrases to give examples Words and phrases to give reasons Appropriate answers
Worksheet 2 **Pages 81–84**	**Descriptions** Speaking Part 2 Linking language Making notes Coherence and fluency
Worksheet 3 **Pages 85–88**	**Discussion topics** Developing ideas Phrases to agree and disagree Developing your ideas

Think about it p89

Extended answer key p98

For useful information about preparing for the IELTS test, go to: weloveielts.org

HOW TO USE THE IELTS BOOSTER

Welcome to the IELTS Booster General Training

What is the IELTS Booster?

The IELTS Booster provides focused test practice on all parts of the IELTS test. It will help you to prepare for the test and gain the confidence, skills and knowledge you need for test day.

How can I use it?

Pick and choose the areas you want to practise at any time.

Use the IELTS Booster alongside a coursebook or on its own as a self-study tool.

Photocopy worksheets to use when you like.

How is it structured?

There are four sections which follow the order of the exam: Listening, Reading, Writing and Speaking.

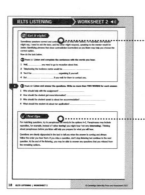

Avoid the most typical mistakes that real IELTS candidates make with *Get it right!* Identify and correct common errors.

Practise vocabulary, grammar or functional language.

Test tips provide practical strategies and advice.

Test facts offer clear, concise information about the exercise type and best ways to approach it.

Access a complete answer key with sample answers for the Writing tasks and audioscript.

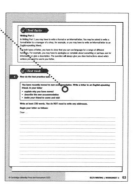

Look at a variety of topics from the test.

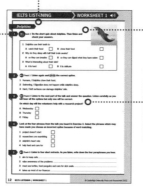

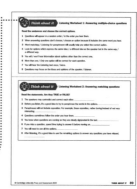

For the audio, scratch the panel to see the code on the inside front cover. Go to cambridgeone.org or scan the QR code.

Find parts and exercises easily. There are several worksheets for each test part.

Think about it exercises help you understand how to approach each question type.

THE IELTS TEST

What are the two types of IELTS test?

The two types of tests are IELTS Academic and IELTS General Training. Both test English language abilities in Listening, Reading, Writing and Speaking. The Listening and Speaking parts are the same for both tests, but the Reading and Writing parts are different.

IELTS Academic is suitable:

- for studying at an English-speaking university, or other higher educational institution, at under- or postgraduate level.
- for professional registration, e.g., to register as an engineer, nurse or accountant in an English-speaking country.

IELTS General Training is suitable:

- for migration to certain English-speaking countries, like Canada or New Zealand.
- for studying below degree level in an English-speaking country.
- for a work placement in an English-speaking country or your own country.

How can I take the IELTS test?

You can take the IELTS test on paper or on a computer.

For IELTS on Paper, the Listening, Reading and Writing are completed on the same day and there are no breaks between them. The Speaking test can be completed up to seven days before or after. The total test time is 2 hours and 45 minutes.

For IELTS on Computer, the content and structure is the same as the paper test. You take the Listening, Reading and Writing test on the computer and the Speaking test is with an examiner face-to-face. The timings are a little different from the paper test as you do not have to transfer your answers to an answer sheet.

For more information about which test is suitable for you, and to check which organisations accept IELTS, go to ielts.org.

Listening 🔊   approximately 30 minutes

Speakers will have a range of native English accents, including British, North American and Australian. You'll hear the listening **once only.**

The Listening has a total of 40 questions and is in four parts. Each part has 10 questions.

Part 1 – a conversation between two people about an everyday topic (e.g., finding out information about a job)

Part 2 – a monologue about an everyday topic (e.g., giving information about changes in a community)

Part 3 – a conversation, usually between two people, in a training or educational context (e.g., students discussing an assignment)

Part 4 – a monologue in an academic context (e.g., a lecture)

Below are the question types you might find in the Listening:

Question type	Task format	Task focus
1 **Multiple choice**	Choose one answer from three alternatives, A–C. Choose two answers from five alternatives, A–E.	Tests detailed understanding of specific points or the overall understanding of the main points.
2 **Matching**	Match a list of statements with a set of options in a box.	Tests the ability to listen for detail and information provided.
3 **Plan, map, diagram labelling**	Label a plan, map or diagram, with a list provided in the question paper.	Tests the ability to understand a description of a place which is represented visually, e.g., the ability to understand and follow directions.
4 **Form, note, table, flowchart, summary completion**	Complete a form, notes, a table, a flowchart or a summary with a word or words from the Listening text.*	Tests the ability to understand and record the main points of the text in different formats.
5 **Sentence completion**	Complete a set of sentences using a word or words from the Listening text.*	Tests the ability to understand the main points in a text, e.g., cause and effect.
6 **Short-answer questions**	Read a question and then answer it with a short answer from the Listening text.*	Tests the ability to understand facts, e.g., places, dates and times.

*Candidates will hear the word they need in the text, and do not need to change it. They will be penalised if they go over the word limit given in the question, e.g., 'Write ONE WORD ONLY for each answer.'

IELTS General Training reading has a total of 40 questions. There are three sections. Section 1 may contain two or three short texts or several shorter texts. Section 2 comprises two texts. In Section 3, there is one long text. Below are the question types you might find:

Question type	Task format	Task focus
1 Multiple choice	Choose one answer from four alternatives, A–D. Choose two answers from five alternatives, A–E. Choose three answers from seven alternatives, A–G.	Tests detailed understanding of specific points or the overall understanding of the main points.
2 Identifying information	Write whether a statement is confirmed (True), states the opposite (False) or is neither confirmed nor contradicted (Not Given).	Tests the ability to identify specific information in a text.
3 Identifying writers' views/claims	Write whether a statement agrees with the claim or view (Yes), disagrees with the claim or view (No), or the claim or view is neither confirmed nor contradicted (Not Given).	Tests the ability to identify ideas and opinions.
4 Matching information	Match information to a paragraph or section of the text.	Tests the ability to scan for specific information in a text.
5 Matching headings	Match headings to the correct paragraph or section. There are always more headings than you need.	Tests the ability to recognise the main topic or idea of a paragraph or section.
6 Matching features	Match pieces of information to a list of options (e.g., match events to historical periods). Some options might not be used.	Tests the ability to scan and to understand facts and opinions in a text.
7 Matching sentence endings	Choose the best way to complete a sentence from a list of options. There are more options than questions.	Tests the ability to understand the main ideas in a text.
8 Sentence completion	Complete a sentence with a word or words from the text.	Tests the ability to find specific information.
9 Summary, note, table, flowchart completion	Complete a summary, notes, a table or a flowchart with a word or words from the text.	Tests the ability to understand details and main ideas of a text.
10 Diagram label completion	Label a diagram with the correct word from the text or list of options.	Tests the ability to understand a description and to transfer information to a diagram.
11 Short answer questions	Read a question and then answer with a short answer from the text.	Tests the ability to understand facts, e.g., places, dates and times.

Correct answers are worth one mark each.

General Training Writing   **60 minutes**

There are two writing tasks, and you must answer both. Aim to take about 20 minutes to answer Task 1 and 40 minutes to answer Task 2.

Task	Number of words	Task format
Writing Task 1	at least 150	You will be presented with a situation and asked to write a letter requesting information or explaining the situation. The letter may be personal, semi-formal or formal in style.
Writing Task 2	at least 250	You will be asked to write an essay in response to a point of view, argument or problem. The essay can be fairly personal in style.

You will be assessed on the following criteria:

Writing Task 1	Task achievement	Coherence and cohesion	Lexical resource	Grammatical range and accuracy
Writing Task 2	Task response	Coherence and cohesion	Lexical resource	Grammatical range and accuracy

Each task is assessed independently. The assessment of Task 2 carries more weight in marking than Task 1.

Speaking   **11–14 minutes**

The test consists of a face-to-face interview with an examiner. Tests are in three parts and are recorded.

Task	Timing	Task format
Speaking Part 1 – Interview	4–5 minutes	You answer questions on familiar topics, e.g., family, hobbies, likes and dislikes.
Speaking Part 2 – Long turn	3–4 minutes (including 1 minute preparation time)	You are given a task card, e.g., 'Describe something you want to own'. You have one minute to make notes before talking for up to two minutes.
Speaking Part 3 – Discussion	4–5 minutes	The examiner will ask you more abstract questions about the topic in Task 2, e.g., 'Does owning lots of possessions make people happy?'

You will be assessed on the following criteria:

Fluency and coherence	Lexical resource	Grammatical range and accuracy	Pronunciation
How well you maintain your flow of speech; how logical your answer is; how well you connect your ideas	The accuracy and variety of the vocabulary you use	The range, accuracy and complexity of the grammar you use	How intelligible you are

HOW IS IELTS SCORED?

You'll be awarded a band score of between 0 and 9 for your overall language ability. In addition, you'll be awarded an individual band score of between 0 and 9 for each of the four skills: Listening, Reading, Writing and Speaking. All scores are recorded on the Test Report Form along with details of your nationality, first language and date of birth. Each of the nine bands corresponds to a descriptive summary of your English language ability:

9 **Expert User** – *has fully operational command of the language. Their use of English is appropriate, accurate and fluent, and shows complete understanding.*

8 **Very Good User** – *has fully operational command of the language with only occasional unsystematic inaccuracies and inappropriate usage. They may misunderstand some things in unfamiliar situations. They handle complex and detailed argumentation well.*

7 **Good User** – *has operational command of the language, though with occasional inaccuracies, inappropriate usage and misunderstandings in some situations. They generally handle complex language well and understand detailed reasoning.*

6 **Competent User** – *has an effective command of the language despite some inaccuracies, inappropriate usage and misunderstandings. They can use and understand fairly complex language, particularly in familiar situations.*

5 **Modest User** – *has a partial command of the language and copes with overall meaning in most situations, although they are likely to make many mistakes. They should be able to handle basic communication in their own field.*

4 **Limited User** – *basic competence is limited to familiar situations. They have frequent problems in understanding and expression. They are not able to use complex language.*

3 **Extremely Limited User** – *conveys and understands only general meaning in very familiar situations. Frequent breakdowns in communication occur.*

2 **Intermittent User** – *has great difficulty understanding spoken and written English.*

1 **Non User** – *essentially has no ability to use the language beyond possibly a few isolated words.*

0 **Did not attempt the test** – *did not answer the questions.*

Dolphins

1 ◀)) Track 1 **Do the short quiz about dolphins. Then listen and check your answers.**

1 Dolphins use their teeth to

   A catch their food ☐   **B** chew their food ☐

2 Why do they sleep with half their brain awake?

   A so they can breathe ☐   **B** so they can digest what they have eaten ☐

3 What is interesting about their skin?

   A it is hard ☐   **B** it is delicate ☐

2 ◀)) Track 1 **Listen again and circle the correct option.**

1 Humans / Dolphins chew their food.

2 Swimming / Digestion does not happen while dolphins sleep.

3 Hard / Soft surfaces can damage dolphins' skin.

3 ◀)) Track 2 **Listen to the next part of the talk and answer the question. Listen carefully as you will hear all the options but only one will be correct.**

On which day will the volunteers help with a research project?

A Wednesday ☐

B Thursday ☐

C Friday ☐

4 **Look at the four phrases from the talk you heard in Exercise 3. Select the phrases which may have made you choose an incorrect option because of word matching.**

1 project doesn't start ☐

2 researchers are examining ☐

3 dolphin's heart rate ☐

4 help feed and care for ☐

5 ◀)) Track 3 **Listen to four short extracts. As you listen, write down the four paraphrases you hear.**

1 aim to keep safe ....

2 raise awareness of the problems ....

3 meet sea turtles, feed penguins and care for sick seals. ....

4 takes up most of our finances ....

6a You are going to listen to the rest of the talk. Before you do, look at the extract below and <u>underline</u> any words that might make you select Option A because of word matching. Option A is one of the options you will be looking at in the next exercise.

Extract: 'It used to be controversial among local experts, but thankfully that's been resolved.'
Option A: Experts do not agree about its value.

6b Look at the extract in Exercise 6a again. Read it carefully and think about meaning. Why is Option A an incorrect option? Discuss with a partner.

7 🔊 Track 4 **Now listen to the rest of the talk.**

What comment is made about each of the following projects?

Choose four comments from the box and write the correct letters (A–F) next to Questions 1–4. Two options are not needed. The questions follow the order you hear them.

Comments	
A Experts do not agree about its value.	**D** It takes quite a long time.
B It is helping future research.	**E** Money is urgently needed.
C It uses new technology.	**F** A lot of volunteers want to do it.

Projects

1 turtle monitoring ....

2 cave mapping ....

3 reef surveying ....

4 beach clear ....

✓ *Test tips*

When answering multiple-choice questions, don't choose an answer because it includes the same word you hear (word matching). Instead look for the option which expresses the same idea as the speaker but in a different way. Note that the questions will appear in the order you hear them.

☑ Test task

8 ◀») Track 5 **Do the test practice task. Listen to a radio interview and answer the questions. Remember to listen for paraphrases and avoid word matching.**

Questions 1 and 2

Choose TWO letters, A–E

Which TWO things does Hannah say about the Dolphin Conservation Trust?

A Children make up most of the membership.

B It is the country's largest conservation organisation.

C It helps finance campaigns for changes in fishing practices.

D It employs several dolphin experts full time.

E Volunteers help in various ways.

....

Questions 3–5

Choose the correct letter, A, B, or C.

3 Why is Hannah so pleased the Trust has won the Charity Commission award?

    A It has brought in extra money.

    B It made the work of the Trust better known.

    C It has attracted more members.

4 Hannah says that a project in Scotland is causing problems for dolphins because of

    A sound.

    B oil leaks.

    C movement of ships.

5 Hannah became interested in dolphins when

    A she saw one swimming near her home.

    B she read a book about them.

    C she heard a speaker at her school.

Questions 6–9

What comment does Hannah make about each of the following dolphins?

Choose FOUR answers from the box and write the correct letter, A–F, next to Questions 6–9.

Two options are not needed. The questions follow the order you hear them.

Comments
A It has a loving personality.
B It is photographed frequently.
C It is always very energetic.
D It has not been seen this year.
E It is the newest to the scheme.
F It has an unusual shape.

Dolphins

6 Moondancer ....

7 Echo ....

8 Kiwi ....

9 Samson ....

Studying and work

A

B

C

1 ▶ Match the photos (A–C) to one of the situations (1–3).

1 studying abroad ....

2 distance learning ....

3 work placement ....

2 ▶ 🔊 Track 6 Listen. Which situation from Exercise 1 does the speaker want to discuss?

....

3 ▶ 🔊 Track 7 Look at the words and think about a suitable paraphrase. Then listen and write down the paraphrases you hear. You can listen more than once.

Advice	
1 find something that is enjoyable	....
2 think about your future goals	....
3 show ability in the subject	....
4 make sure you work hard	....
5 get help	....

4 ▶ Look at the questions (1–5) and <u>underline</u> the words you think will be signposted in the listening text. The first one has been done for you.

Stages in doing a year abroad

1 in the <u>second year</u> of the course

2 when first choosing where to go

3 when sending your choices

4 when writing your personal statement

5 when doing the year abroad

5 ▶ 🔊 Track 8 Listen to the short excerpt from a conversation between two students, Mia and Josh. Which question from Exercise 4 is Mia talking about?

6 ◀))) Track 9 **Now listen to the first part of the same conversation and choose the correct option. Remember to listen carefully as soon as you hear the words that tell you (signpost) when the answer is coming.**

1 In the second year of the course Josh should

   A make travel arrangements and bookings.

   B show ability in Theatre Studies.

7a **You are going to listen to the whole conversation between Mia and Josh. Before you listen, look at the remaining options and write down the paraphrases you might hear. B has been done for you.**

Actions	
A make travel arrangements and bookings	....
B show ability in Theatre Studies	*get good marks and know the subject well* ....
C be on time	....
D get a letter of recommendation	....
E plan for the final year	....
F make sure the focus of the course is relevant	....
G ask for help	....

7b ◀))) Track 10 **Now listen. Choose FOUR answers from the box in Exercise 7a and write the correct letter next to Questions 2–5. Remember there will always be options that you do not need. Question 1 has been done for you.**

Stages in doing a 'year abroad'

1 in the second year of the course   .B......

2 when choosing where to go   ....

3 when sending your choices   ....

4 when writing your personal statement   ....

5 when doing the year abroad   ....

Get it right!

Sometimes speakers correct and contradict each as they offer advice. For example, one speaker might say, *I need to ask the tutor*, and the other might respond, *speaking to the mentor would be better*. Identifying phrases that show contradiction (correction) as you listen may help you choose the correct option.

Now do the task below.

🔊 **Track 11 Listen and complete the sentences with the words you hear.**

1 Well, ... you need to go to reception about that.

2 Telephoning the business centre would be ....

3 You'd be .... organising it yourself.

4 But .... if you wait for them to contact you.

8 🔊 **Track 12 Listen and answer the questions. Write no more than TWO WORDS for each answer. Compare your answers with a partner.**

1 Who should help with the assignment? ....

2 How should the student get more information? ....

3 Who should the student speak to about her accommodation? ....

4 What should the student do about her application? ....

☑ Test tips

For matching questions, try to paraphrase the words in the options A–E. Paraphrases may include opposites, for example, instead of 'rather **boring**' you might hear 'not very **interesting**'. Thinking about paraphrases before you listen will help you prepare for what you will hear.

Questions are clearly signposted in the text to tell you when the answer is coming and always follow the order you hear them. If you miss a question, don't stop listening but continue to the next question. At the end of the listening, you may be able to answer any questions that you missed from the remaining options.

Test task

9 ⏵ 🔊 Track 13 **Do the test practice task. Listen to the conversation about work placement and answer the questions. What source of information should Alex use at each of the following stages of the work placement?**

Choose SIX answers from the box and write the correct letter, A–G, next to Questions 1–6.

Stages of the work placement

A get updates

B discuss options

C supply a reference

D informing about outcome of interview

E responding to invitation for interview

F obtain company information

G register with STEP

Sources of information

1 careers officer ....

2 work experience fair ....

3 the internet ....

4 mentor ....

5 human resources department ....

6 personal tutor ....

Films and filmmaking

1 🔊 **Track 14 What do you know about films and filmmaking? Complete the short quiz with a partner, then listen and check your answers. You can listen more than once.**

1 A 'mainstream' film can be described as

A a film with lots of special effects. ☐

B a film made by a large production company. ☐

2 What type of films enter film festival competitions?

A independent films ☐

B studio films ☐

3 Most studio films are funded by

A private investors and individuals. ☐

B the studio that is making them. ☐

4 Film production consists of

A seven stages. ☐

B ten stages. ☐

2 **Look at the flowchart opposite and answer the questions with no more than TWO WORDS. Do not fill in the gaps in the flowchart just yet.**

1 What process is being described? ....

2 How many steps are there in the process? ....

3 Do you need to answer a question in each stage? ....

4 For the third gap, do you need a singular or plural noun?..

Video animation process

Hold a meeting with the **1** ....

⬇

Create a video **2** .... and write the script.

⬇

Go online and find an actor with a suitable **3** ....

⬇

Produce a storyboard using **4** .... of the stages of the story.

⬇

Develop the visual style by including **5** .... and background images.

⬇

Do the animation to add life to the images.

⬇

To create mood, add **6** ....

3 🔊 Track 15 **Listen to the first part of a conversation between two students, Ria and Stan. As you listen, fill in the first gap (1) in the flowchart in Exercise 2. Write ONE WORD ONLY.**

4 🔊 Track 15 **Listen again. What words do you hear that tell you the answer is coming?**

A Have you got a minute? ☐

B I'm not too sure about all the stages. ☐

C The first thing is … ☐

5 🔊 Track 16 **Now listen to the whole conversation between Ria and Stan, and fill in the remaining gaps (2–6) in the flowchart in Exercise 2. Write ONE WORD ONLY for each answer.**

6 🔊 Track 16 **Ria and Stan use signposting language which will help you follow what they are saying. Complete the sentences from the conversation with the words in the box. Then listen to the conversation from Exercise 5 again and check your answers.**

finish	following	move	once	that	then

1 Next, we .... on to the idea or concept stage.

2 Then, ... that's been agreed, we start writing the script.

3 We .... have to find an actor.

4 After .... , a storyboard is put together.

5 The .... step, animation, is probably my favourite.

6 Before we .... , we can set the mood by adding the right music.

7 Track 17 **Listen to the extracts and complete the sentences with ONE WORD ONLY.**

1 To .... this point, let me tell you about what I did at the film studio.

2 This brings me to my .... point, which is the development of special effects.

3 So, in other .... , the reason I chose film studies was because …

4 OK, so we've .... at the challenges of scriptwriting …

5 I'd like to .... by describing the film production process.

6 I've .... about the role of the director …

☑ *Test tips*

When giving a presentation or lecture, speakers often use signposting language to connect their ideas and move between topics. Listening for signposting language as well as using the headings and subheadings on the question paper will help you follow the speaker and answer the questions correctly.

---

8 **Match the extracts (1–6) in Exercise 7 to their uses (A–D) below.**

A to start a new topic   ....

B to give an example   ....

C to paraphrase and clarify   ....

D to finish a topic   ....

Test task

🔊 **Track 18 Listen to a presentation about film production and complete the flowchart below. Write ONE WORD ONLY for each answer. Remember, listen for signposting and use the subheadings to help you follow the speaker.**

The stages of film production

Development

Projects begin with development of a **1** .... based on a book or other source. Writers produce an outline.

⬇

Pre-production

Production options are reduced and **2** .... starts.

3 .... are employed.

⬇

Production

A schedule must be followed so there are no problems with the **4** ....

5 .... is very important.

⬇

Photography

An expensive stage because of things like **6** .... and filming in

7 .... places.

⬇

Wrap

The set is taken down, the site cleared, and goods are returned to **8** ....

⬇

Postproduction

Film footage is in the **9** ....

⬇

Distribution

Producers recover their investments. Films are sent to **10** .... or online platforms.

Maps

1 Look at the photos (A–C) and match them to the most appropriate sentences (1–3).

A    B    C

1 Take the left fork. ....

2 Follow the road, round the bend. ....

3 Turn right at the junction. ....

2a 🔊 Track 19 **Look at the three maps (A, B and C). Listen and decide which map shows the directions that the speaker gives.**

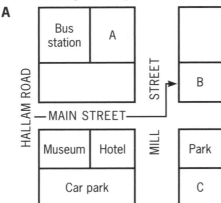

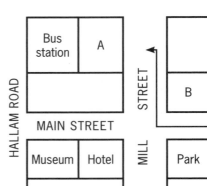

2b 🔊 Track 19 **Listen again and complete the phrases. Use no more than THREE WORDS.**

1 Right. Well, ... Main Street.

2 .... at the lights.

3 It's .... the park.

⊚ *Get it right!*

For map labelling questions, you will need to understand and follow directions. Familiarising yourself with the language of location and direction will help you follow the speaker.

🔊 **Track 20 Complete the phrases with the words in the box. Then listen and check your answers.**

alongside	before	centre	over	rear	round	through	up

1 Walk .... this road until you reach the lights.

2 Go .... the door on the right.

3 Just .... the bend you will find the coffee shop.

4 Go .... the bridge and into the forest.

5 Enter via the .... of the building.

6 You'll find the fountain in the .... of the park.

7 Just .... you reach the lake, there is the picnic area.

8 The river runs .... the railway line.

3 🔊 **Track 21 Look at the map and the candidate's answers. The candidate has answered two questions incorrectly and one correctly. Listen and put a tick (✓) next to the correct answer and write the correct letter (A–G) next to the incorrect answers. Compare your answers with a partner.**

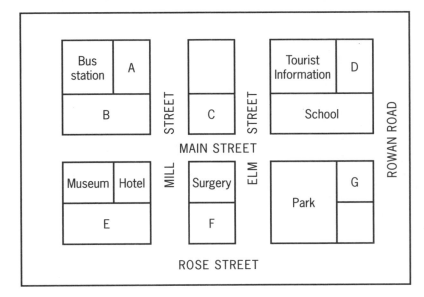

1 bank ....D............   2 coffee shop ....C............   3 science centre ....A............

4 🔊 **Track 22 Listen to extracts from a talk about planned improvements to a town called Red Hill. Correct the underlined words with what the speaker actually says.**

1 The trees will be located <u>opposite</u> the supermarket. ....

2 Pavements <u>at the junction of</u> Carberry Street … ....

3 Traffic lights will be installed <u>at the end of</u> Hill Street. ....

5 🔊 **Track 23 The map below shows the planned improvements to Red Hill. Listen and write the correct letters (A–H) next to Questions 1–7. The questions follow the order of the talk. There is one letter you do not need.**

Red Hill Improvement Plan

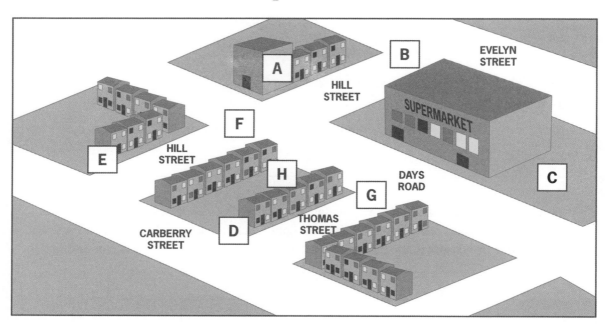

1 trees ....

2 wider pavements ....

3 painted road surface ....

4 new sign ....

5 traffic lights ....

6 paintings ....

7 children's playground ....

Test tips

If you are given a compass icon showing north, south, east and west, it is likely you will hear phrases like 'in the west' and 'to the south'. Use them to help orientate and direct you.

6 ▶ **Look at the map below. Complete the sentences with the correct phrases.**

| in the far northwest in the southeast just on the west near the north south of to the east |

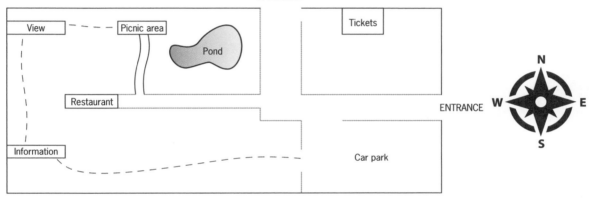

1 The car park is .... corner.

2 There's a viewpoint .... of the park.

3 .... of the viewpoint, you'll find the picnic area.

4 A little .... the picnic area, past the fishpond, is the restaurant.

5 There's a small path, ... edge of car park which goes to the information centre.

6 .... entrance is the ticket office.

☑ *Test task*

7 🔊 **Track 24 Label the map below. Listen and write the correct letters (A–I) next to Questions 1–5.**

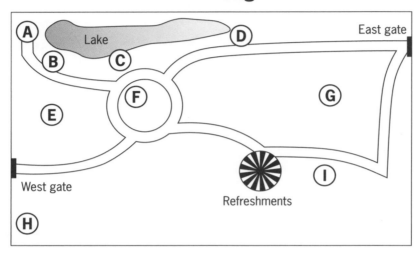

Hinchingbrooke Park

1 bird hide   ....

2 dog walking   ....

3 flower garden   ....

4 wood   ....

5 toilets   ....

Animals in the wild

1 🔊 Track 25 **Look at the photos.**

What do you think the animals have in common? Discuss with a partner.

....

Listen to the beginning of a conversation between Kennie and Anna, and check your ideas.

🎯 Get it right!

In IELTS Listening, candidates often lose marks because they have made simple mistakes, for example, they have ignored the word limit or they have not checked whether a singular or plural noun form is needed. Make sure you read instructions carefully, use headings (if there are any) and check your answers before you transfer them to the answer sheet.

a Look at the table and instructions. Four of the answers (1–6) are incorrect because the candidate has made simple mistakes and two are correct. Put a cross (✗) next to the candidate's 'incorrect' answers and a tick (✓) next to the correct ones.

Write NO MORE THAN TWO WORDS for each answer.

Tilly's Tours			
Day	**Event**	**Venue**	**Information**
Monday	**1** The river walk	Central Park	There is a **2** small £10 charge
Tuesday	**3** Wednesday	Gallery	There are no **4** camera allowed
5 Saturday	Whale watching	Aquarium	Children cannot feed **6** the animals

b Now match the common candidate errors in the table with the reasons for the errors (A–C) below.

A The candidate did not follow the instructions. ....

B The candidate did not write the exact word they heard. ....

C The candidate did not use the headings to help them. ....

2 ▶ Delete the incorrect option.

1 Leylah wants to buy these book / books for her IELTS class.

2 I have some concern / concerns about the test.

3 Either boy / boys can help you paint the door.

4 I'm not sure if both girl / girls went to school yesterday.

5 When she went on holiday to Rome, she visited a number of museum / museums.

6 That's the third time this week! Why do you arrive late every day / days?

7 He's in the park with one of his dog / dogs now.

8 It's time we started to protect these animal / animals.

9 I have several idea / ideas to share with you.

10 That was the main thing / things I wanted to tell you.

3 ▶ Look at the table in Exercise 4 and read the instructions and headings carefully. Ask yourself one or two questions using the information on either side of the gaps and write them down. Use the question words 'What', 'Why', 'Where', 'Who', etc. Examples for the first two have been done for you.

1 _What part of a shark (noun) might a pattern cover? What part of a shark might help it move easily?_

2 _Where might part of a shark be used by humans?_

3 ....

4 ....

5 ....

6 ....

4 ▶ 🔊 Track 26 Now listen to the whole conversation between Kennie and Anna that you heard the beginning of in Exercise 1. As you listen, complete the table. Remember to use the headings and information provided to help you follow the speakers and hear the correct answers. Write ONE WORD ONLY for each answer.

Animal	Reasons for scientific interest	Human use
Shark	A pattern covering its **1** .... helps it move easily.	Used on the bottom of **2** ....
Gecko	**3** .... on their feet allow them to stick to smooth surfaces.	**4** .... have been made for climbers. Plans for use in space.
Kingfisher	Aerodynamic: They can **5** .... silently because of the shape of their beak.	Japanese high-speed trains are quiet in **6** ....

Test tips

When answering table completion questions, use the time before you listen to look at the instructions and headings, and think about the type of words (or numbers) you are listening for. Asking yourself questions, using the information on either side of the gap (if there is any), might increase your understanding and help you hear the correct answer when you listen.

Test task

5 🔊 **Track 27 Questions 1–7. Listen and complete the table below.**

Write ONE WORD ONLY for each answer.

Animals	Reasons for population increase in gardens	Comments
1	Appropriate stretches of water	Massive increase in urban population
Hedgehogs	Safer from **2** .... in cities	Easy to **3** .... them accurately
Song thrushes	A variety of **4** .... to eat More nesting places available	A large **5** .... starting soon
Peregrine falcon	Less use of **6**	Possible to watch them **7** ....

Design competition

1 ◀)) Track 28 Read the dos and don'ts, and predict a suitable word for each gap. Then listen and check your answers.

Note completion

Do

1 Use any headings to .... you follow the speaker.

2 Think about the type of .... you need, for example a place.

3 Listen for specific ....

4 Remember the answers will come in the .... you hear them.

Don't

5 Waste .... as you are listening.

6 Leave any question .... : guess if you are not sure.

7 .... anything the speaker says, for example write 'frog' if you hear 'frogs'.

---

2 ◀)) Track 28 Listen again and write the paraphrases or synonyms you hear for these phrases.

1 use the headings

   ....

2 think about

   ....

3 remember that the answers

   ....

4 as you are listening

   ....

5 if you are not sure

   ....

3 Which phrase told you the speaker was moving to the final point. Choose the correct option.

A right, next I'd say ☐

B one more thing ☐

C that's a big mistake ☐

4 ▸ Look at the <u>underlined</u> words and write down synonyms or paraphrases you might hear. The first one has been done for you. Don't worry about the answering the questions (1–5) yet.

Global Design Competition

Jonas's **1** .... told Jonas to <u>get help</u>. <u>find support</u>...........

The professor has received Jonas's **2** .... <u>by email</u>. ....

Jonas is <u>designing a device</u> that can be used at home in a **3** ....

Jonas aims to use **4** .... <u>in a new way</u>. ....

Jonas believes **5** .... are <u>similar</u> and <u>not very interesting</u>.

....

5 ▸ Look at the sentences in Exercise 4 again. Predict what type of word is needed in each gap and write it down. The first one has been done for you.

Sentence 1   <u>a person</u>...

Sentence 2   ....

Sentence 3   ....

Sentence 4   ....

Sentence 5   ....

6a ▸ Look at an excerpt from the listening. <u>Underline</u> the word in the excerpt that fits in the first gap in Exercise 4.

JONAS: Hello professor. I'm working on my entry for the Global Design Competition.

My tutor said you might be able to give me some support.

6b ▸ 🔊 Track 29 **Now listen and complete the sentences (2–5) in Exercise 4 with ONE WORD only. Write down the exact word you hear and remember the questions follow the order of the conversation.**

Test tips

Before you listen, look at the questions and consider what paraphrases or synonyms you might hear. Identifying paraphrases as you listen will help you 'hear' when the correct answer is coming.

 Test task

7 🔊 Track 30 **Listen to the final part of Jonas's conversation with his professor and complete the notes below.**

Write ONE WORD ONLY for each answer.

Global Design Competition

'The Rockpool'

- The stone in Jonas's design is used for **1** .... the machine.
- Carbon dioxide is used to **2** .... the dishes.
- At the end of the washing cycle, **3** .... goes into a holding chamber.
- Jonas thinks his idea has a lot of **4** .... to reduce household costs.

Entry submission

- Jonas needs help preparing for his **5** ....
- The professor advises Jonas to make a **6** .... of his design.
- Jonas's main problem is getting good quality **7** ....
- The professor suggests Jonas apply for a **8** ....
- The professor will check the **9** .... in Jonas's written report.

Read quickly through the following text and scan the questions. Don't worry about answering the questions yet.

Juicers

Are you a keen to have a healthy diet? Then why not buy a juicer so you can blend fruits or vegetables together to make fresh, healthy drinks?

A Citrus Heaven

If you're looking for a reasonably priced juicer for blending your favourite citrus fruits or green vegetables, then this budget model is ideal. While it doesn't win first prize for its looks, it does have a space-saving design, which means it's tall rather than bulky. All its key parts come apart for washing by hand but be warned – they can be stiff to remove on occasion.

B Mean Greens

This isn't the cheapest juicer around but it has a long list of capabilities and is able to tackle all kinds of fruit and vegetables easily. It's on the large size though, so unless you have a kitchen to match, consider another model. Each of its parts is dishwasher friendly and it's quiet too – unlike some other models which sounded a bit like a small jet taking off! Choose from cool blue or bright pink.

C Fruit Shoot

If you lack space in your kitchen and you're after a juicer to do the basics like juicing your oranges for breakfast time, then you need look no further. Our juicer has been built to stand the test of time and it has already survived four years of daily use. The parts need to be washed in the sink, but they'll come out gleaming. It's a bit loud though, so keep the door shut when you're using it. It comes in black or grey.

D Juice Rite

This juicer works well with soft fruits like apricots and tangerines, but less so with leafy greens – so if you're a green vegetable juice lover, look elsewhere! It will fit neatly on your worktop and comes in bright yellow, red, blue or green. The cutting blades need hand washing, but the rest of the parts are dishwasher safe.

E Citrus Blitz

This juicer is pricey but it's a thing of beauty with its stylish curved lines. It's available in a choice of two colours – we liked the pale blue one best – and it's compact enough to keep on the worktop. An added bonus is that it hardly makes a sound when it's juicing. If you're a fan of freshly squeezed juice in the morning, this is a good investment.

F Pulp It

This pastel green juicer is simple to use, juicing your oranges, lemons, limes and other citrus fruits in next to no time. And the noise is minimal compared with other juicers too. You even get a few accessories thrown in – there's a special cleaning brush for washing each of its parts by hand, and there's a smoothie and ice cream strainer too.

Look at the reviews for juicers. For which juicer are the following statements true? NB You may use any letter more than once.

1   It is available in a range of different colours.   ....
2   It is noisy when in use.   ....
3   It costs less than some other juicers.   ....
4   All its parts can go in the dishwasher.   ....
5   It is particularly attractive.   ....
6   It takes up a lot of space.   ....
7   Some extras are included.   ....
8   It is designed to last a long time.   ....

1 ⟩ Match the items in the checklist below with the statements 1–8 in the task above. The first one has been done for you. There is an extra item that you do not need to use.

Buying a juicer – checklist of things to consider

Cost = ...3...   Colour = ...

Method of cleaning = ...   Level of noise = ...

Speed = ...   Appearance = ...

Durability (how long it will   Size = ...

last) = ...   Extras = ...

2 ⟩ Choose the correct paraphrase for these phrases from the text. Discuss your answers with a partner.

1   reasonably priced
    A   costs a lot   ☐   B   not too expensive   ☐
2   it wins first prize for its looks
    A   it looks great   ☐   B   it's not attractive   ☐
3   built to stand the test of time
    A   should continue to work for years   ☐   B   may need replacing before long   ☐
4   comes in black or grey
    A   available in several different colours   ☐   B   there's a choice of two colours   ☐
5   not dishwasher friendly
    A   can be placed in the dishwasher   ☐   B   must be washed by hand   ☐
6   It hardly makes a sound
    A   it's quiet   ☐   B   it's noisy   ☐
7   compact
    A   quite big   ☐   B   small and neat   ☐
8   in next to no time
    A   fast   ☐   B   slow   ☐

3 Read Statement 1 from the reading task carefully and look at the <u>underlined</u> phrase.

It is available in a <u>range of different colours</u>.

Which best describes the <u>underlined</u> phrase?

A one colour   **B** two colours   **C** three colours or more

Now read the whole text quickly and find FIVE sentences in paragraphs A–F that mention colour. <u>Underline</u> the colours mentioned in the five paragraphs.

Look at each of these five paragraphs more closely. Which ONE mentions a range of different colours? Choose your answer and then check in the answer key.

4 Read Statement 2 in the reading task and <u>underline</u> the key words. Find THREE paragraphs that mention the level of noise and <u>underline</u> areas of text that describe this. Read these texts carefully and choose your answer.

5 Follow the same procedure to complete the remaining statements (3–8).

Test tip

Matching statements

In this type of task, you get a list of statements and you have to match each statement to a thing, a person or a place. In this task, the questions will not be in the same order as the text. You will need to jump around rather than reading from beginning to end.

 **Test task**

6 **Do the test practice task. Read the text below and answer Questions 1–8.**

Intercity Sleeper between London and Scotland

Most tickets may be used for travel by Sleeper, subject to availability, and a reservation in a two-berth cabin can be made for £25, except in the case of Solo and Special tickets, which include Sleeper reservations in the fare. The price includes early morning tea or coffee and biscuits. A continental or hot breakfast can be ordered if you wish.

Choose from a range of tickets to suit your journey.

A SuperApex

Only available for travel after 9am. Book at least 2 weeks ahead and travel between Edinburgh or Glasgow and London for the unbeatable price of £59 return. This ticket is non-refundable unless the service is cancelled.

B Apex

A real bargain fare. Only £69 return between Edinburgh or Glasgow and London. Great value Sleeper travel available by booking at least a week before outward travel. Ticket refundable on payment of a 25% administrative charge.

C SuperSaver

Available right up to the day of travel and valid any day except these peak days: all Fridays, also 18–30 December, 31 March and 28 May. Departures between midnight and 2am count as previous day's departures. London to Glasgow or Edinburgh £82.

D Saver

This flexible ticket is valid every day and can be bought on the day of travel. Your ticket allows standard class travel on any train between 10am and midnight. No seat reservations available. London to Glasgow or Edinburgh £95.

E Solo

Treat yourself and enjoy exclusive use of a Standard cabin. Solo is an inclusive return travel ticket with Sleeper reservations for one or both directions. Outward and return reservations should be made at the time of booking. The journey must include a Saturday night away. £140–160 London to Edinburgh/Glasgow return.

F Special

Special is an inclusive return travel package for two people including Sleeper reservations for one or both directions. It can mean savings for both of you. Outward and return reservations should be made at the time of booking. From £120.

G Standard

Not the cheapest option but available up to the time of travel and valid for all trains and at all times. You are advised to turn up early for travel on a Friday.

Look at the seven types of train ticket, A–G.

For which type of train ticket are the following statements true?

Write the correct letter, A–G.

NB You may use any letter more than once.

1 There are advantages if you book a journey with a friend.
2 You cannot use this on a Friday.
3 This can be used without restriction.
4 This can only be booked up to 7 days before departure.
5 It's the cheapest ticket available but there is a restriction on departure time.
6 If you decide not to travel after you have bought the ticket, you cannot get your money back.
7 This is not available if you're travelling out on a Monday and back the next day.
8 You cannot use this ticket for departures between midnight and 10am.

Read quickly through the following text and scan the questions.

Tiritiri Matangi Island Day Trip – New Zealand

Overview

Tiritiri Matangi island is a protected sanctuary for rare and endangered animal and bird species of New Zealand. It is home to many native birds, including the colourful takahe, and the New Zealand robin and fernbird. You will have the day to explore the area, where visitor numbers are limited in order to protect the island's wildlife.

What to expect

You will enjoy a 75-minute ferry ride from Auckland across the Hauraki Gulf to the harbour of the reserve. On arrival you will be met by the island's ranger and volunteer guides. You will receive a short orientation, where you will learn about the deforestation of the island and environmental recovery efforts since 1984, which have helped re-establish 12 endangered native bird species and three reptile species, including the rare tuatara – a prehistoric lizard.

You can then opt to take a 1.5-hour guided walk, which is recommended for an in-depth introduction to the island's wildlife and history, or you can choose to spend the whole day exploring the island on your own.

The guided walk will finish at the visitor centre, where you can browse through informative, interactive exhibits. Complimentary tea and coffee is provided at the centre and there are plenty of tables where you can eat your lunch (not sold on the island so please bring your own). Afterwards, you can relax on the grounds outside the visitor centre and perhaps check out the island's lighthouse. With its 77 steps, it was once the brightest lighthouse in the southern hemisphere. Alternatively, you can explore the walking trails that wind throughout the island, with varying choices for the whole range of fitness levels and experience.

Additional information

Please bring suitable walking shoes, a light raincoat, sunscreen and a hat.

Read the questions but don't worry about doing this exercise yet.

Questions 1–8

Do the following statements agree with the information given in the text?

Write
TRUE   *if the statement agrees with the information*
FALSE   *if the statement contradicts the information*
NOT GIVEN *if there is no information on this*

1   Restrictions apply to the number of visitors permitted on the island.
2   The orientation is provided by the ranger.
3   The tuatara lizard is now only found on this island.
4   Participants are expected to join the walking tour.
5   Trip participants are allowed to touch the displays in the visitor centre.
6   Food is available for participants to purchase on the island.
7   Participants have the opportunity to climb to the top of the lighthouse.
8   Some trails are suitable for inexperienced walkers.

1 **Read the reading task as quickly as you can. Which paragraph (1–5) contains the following information?**

1 Details about the lighthouse ....
2 Advice about items of clothing and footwear to bring on the trip ....
3 Examples of bird species to be seen on the island ....
4 Refreshments available in the visitor centre ....
5 Information about walking trails ....
6 Details of the orientation given to visitors ....

2 **Find the answers to these questions are quickly as you can.**

1 How long does the guided walk take to complete? ....
2 How long is the ferry ride to the island? ....
3 How many reptile species can be seen on the island? ....
4 How many steps does the lighthouse have? ....
5 When did conservation efforts begin on the island? ....

Test tip

Key words

The statements will be in text order. They will often contain words that come from the text so that you know what part of the text you need to read carefully to find the answer. Scan the text to find the paragraph which contains the key word or words given in the statement.

3a **Read the first three statements in the reading task and <u>underline</u> the key words in each one. The first one has been done for you.**

3b **<u>Underline</u> the parts of the text which relate to Statements 1–3.**

3c **Read Paragraphs 1 and 2 carefully, and the areas of text around the words and phrases you <u>underlined</u>. Match each statement with an answer. One answer is TRUE, two answers are NOT GIVEN. Then check your answers in the answer key.**

Test tip

NOT GIVEN statements

NOT GIVEN statements are often based on information you might expect to be in the text but is not. They often contain some words that appear in the text itself. Read each statement and the relevant part of the text very carefully before deciding whether the idea is given or not. Make sure you know what is being referred to in the text.

3d Why might some candidates think that the two NOT GIVEN statements are true?

....

....

4a Read the remaining statements (4–7) and <u>underline</u> the key words and phrases. Locate these in the text.

4b Then match each statement with an answer.

☑ Test task

5 Do the test practice task. Read the text below and answer Questions 1–7.

Smoke alarms in the home

Smoke alarms are now a standard feature in Australian homes and are required by the National Building Code in any recently built properties. They are installed to detect the presence of smoke and emit a clear sound to alert you in the event of fire to give you time to escape.

There are two principal types of smoke alarms. Ionization alarms are the cheapest and most readily available smoke alarms. They are also very sensitive to 'flaming fires' – fires that burn fiercely – and will detect them before the smoke gets too thick. However, photoelectric alarms are more effective at detecting slow-burning fires. They are less likely to go off accidentally and so are best for homes with one floor. For the best protection, you should install one of each.

Most battery-powered smoke alarms can be installed by the homeowner and do not require professional installation. For the installation of hard-wired smoke alarms, powered from the mains electricity supply, however, you will need the services of a licensed professional. Smoke alarms are usually most effective when located on the ceiling, near or in the middle of the room or hall.

Photoelectric smoke alarms in any quantity may be disposed of in domestic waste. If you have fewer than ten ionization alarms to get rid of, you may put them in your domestic waste. If you have more than ten to dispose of, you should contact your local council.

Your battery-powered smoke alarm will produce a short beep every 60 seconds to alert you when the battery is running out and needs replacing. Nevertheless, it should be tested every month to ensure that the battery and the alarm sounder are working. Note that the sensitivity in all smoke alarms will reduce over time.

Do the following statements agree with the information given in the text?

Write
TRUE   *if the statement agrees with the information*
FALSE   *if the statement contradicts the information*
NOT GIVEN *if there is no information on this*

1 All new houses in Australia must have smoke alarms.
2 Photoelectric smoke alarms cost less than ionization smoke alarms.
3 It takes a short time to fit most smoke alarms.
4 Any hard-wired smoke alarm must be fitted by a specialist technician.
5 You should get in touch with your local council before placing any ionization smoke alarms in household rubbish.
6 Smoke alarms give a warning sound to indicate that battery power is low.
7 Smoke alarms need to be checked on a fortnightly basis.

Read quickly through the following text and scan the questions.

Working as a greenkeeper – Western Australia

What they do

Greenkeepers plant and maintain the grass used for public parks, gardens and sporting areas. They sow grass seeds and lay turf: the short grass and the surface of soil used to make lawns. They mow the grass, trim plants and fertilise the soil.

They undertake repairs and maintenance of metal gates, wooden fences and gravel paths, and ensure the grounds remain tidy and totally free of debris. They mark out and prepare sporting areas such as football pitches, running tracks and golf courses.

Working conditions

Greenkeepers mostly work outdoors in all weather. However, they may also spend some of their time indoors in an office doing some administrative tasks. They may work long hours every day. This may involve starting very early in the morning and continuing late into the evening.

Machinery and technologies

Greenkeepers use lawnmowers and other machinery, such as leaf-blowers. They occasionally also operate a mini tractor in their work. They wear protective footwear and overalls as well as gloves and goggles if using toxic chemicals to minimise any associated risks. They need to be competent in the use of computers and may need to use specialised business management software packages.

How do I become one?

Education and training

It is possible to work as a greenkeeper without formal qualifications; however, skills in turf management or horticulture are usually required. You may be able to gain these skills through work experience in a related role.

You can also undertake an apprenticeship in turf management. This usually takes 48 months to complete. Traineeships in sports turf management are also offered at colleges and other training organisations throughout Western Australia. These take 12 months to complete. As an apprentice or trainee, you enter into a formal training contract with an employer. You will spend time working and learning practical skills on the job, and you spend some time undertaking structured training with a registered training provider.

Entry into this occupation will be improved by obtaining a qualification in horticulture.

Read the questions but don't worry about doing this exercise yet.

Questions 1–9

Choose ONE WORD AND/OR A NUMBER from the text for each answer.

1 Greenkeepers are responsible for mending timber ....
2 It is important for greenkeepers to ensure that all .... is removed from the grounds.
3 A greenkeeper ensures that grounds such as soccer .... are ready for use.
4 Greenkeepers mainly carry out their duties ....
5 .... as well as manual work may be carried out by greenkeepers.
6 The work of a greenkeeper sometimes involves driving a small ....
7 When handling dangerous .... , special hand protection must be worn by greenkeepers.
8 The normal duration of a traineeship is ....
9 Someone who has a relevant .... may have a better chance of getting a job as a greenkeeper.

1 Look at the picture of a greenkeeper and read the sentences below. Complete each sentence with the correct word from the underlined pairs of words below.

Greenkeepers

1 look after a range of green area / spaces.   ....
2 do all their work / duty in the open air.   ....
3 work long hours / time on a daily basis.   ....
4 use a variety of tool / machines and equipment.   ....
5 never need to wear special clothes / garment.   ....
6 must have a qualification / training.   ....

2 Read the text as quickly as you can. Are the sentences in Exercise 1 true or false according to the information in the text? Write T for TRUE or F for FALSE next to each one. Underline the areas of text that give you the answers.

3 Match the words and phrases from the text with the paraphrases (a–g).

1 sow	a eye protection
2 trim	b to have a good working knowledge of
3 undertake	c dangerous
4 gravel	d take responsibility for
5 goggles	e job
6 toxic	f small stones
7 to be competent in	g cut
8 occupation	h plant

4a Read Sentences 1–9 carefully and <u>underline</u> words and phrases before and after the gaps. This will help you decide what kind of word you need to write in the gaps.

4b Now write the sentence numbers (1–9) in the gaps below.

Which sentences need

- a word and a number?   ....
- a singular noun?   ....
- an adjective?   ....
- an adverb?   ....
- a plural noun?   ....

5 Look at the students' answers for Sentence 1. Both answers are incorrect. Why?

Adam: *fence*   **Beatrice:** *gates*

6 Read the text carefully and complete Sentences 1–9.

Test tip

Sentence completion

It is important to read the sentence very carefully and pay particular attention to the type of word you need to look for in the text. The completed sentence must be correct grammatically and the meaning of the sentence must match the meaning of the text.

7 Do the test practice task. Read the text below and answer Questions 1–6.

JLP Retail: Staff benefits

Pay

Whatever your role, your pay range will be extremely competitive and reviewed in the light of your progress. In addition to your salary, you will enjoy an array of excellent benefits from the moment you join the company.

Holiday

The holiday entitlement is four weeks per year, rising to five weeks after three years (or, in the case of IT graduate trainees, after promotion to programmer or trainee analyst).

Pension scheme

We offer a non-contributory final salary pension scheme, payable from the age of 60 to most staff who have completed the qualifying period of five years. Our life assurance scheme pays a sum equivalent to three times your annual salary to your nominated beneficiary.

Holiday and leisure facilities

The business owns a number of residential clubs which offer subsidised holiday accommodation for staff with at least three years' service.

Sports clubs

We support an extensive range of sports activities including football, netball, golf, skiing, sailing, squash, riding and gliding.

Subsidies

Ticket subsidies of 50% of the cost of plays or concerts are available. Staff may also take advantage of corporate membership to bodies such as the Science Museum. We give generous financial support to staff who wish to acquire leisure skills or continue their education, e.g. through the Open University or evening classes.

Financial help, benefits and discounted deals

In cases of particular hardship, we will help staff with a loan. We have also negotiated a range of benefits for staff such as discounted private health care and a car purchase scheme, along with a number of one-off deals with hotels and amusement parks.

Questions 1–6

Complete the sentences below.

Choose NO MORE THAN TWO WORDS AND/OR A NUMBER from the text for each answer.

1 Pay increases depend on the .... that each member of staff makes.
2 Employees must work a minimum of .... to be eligible for a pension.
3 Staff may take a holiday at one of the .... provided by the company.
4 The company pays half the seat price for .... and plays.
5 The company gives financial assistance for both educational courses and .... as part of staff development.
6 Employees may be entitled to a .... if they find themselves in difficult circumstances.

Read quickly through the following text and scan the questions.

The mystery of the incredible human brain

Throughout the day, different parts of your body clamour to be heard. You run too fast for the bus, and your heart is pounding – telling you to slow down and wait for the next one. But what about your brain? When was the last time you sat in a quiet, darkened room with no distractions and allowed your brain to think about itself? Maybe you never have.

Despite some remarkable advances, the brain remains largely a mystery. We know an adult brain weighs about 1.3 kilograms; it's pink and wrinkly and feels a bit like a mushroom. We also know the brain is made up of about 100 billion nerve cells, called 'neurons', connected like wires in a telephone exchange. Messages pass down them like electric signals and are carried from one neuron to the next by neurotransmitter chemicals. We even know where many different brain functions, such as memory and smell, reside. But what we don't really understand yet is the link between the micro and the macro: how the pattern of electrical and chemical signals results in things like consciousness, intelligence and creativity.

Much of our knowledge comes from studying brain function when things go wrong. One of the most famous cases was an American railroad worker called Phineas Gage. Some 150 years ago, he was using a metal rod to pack gunpowder into a hole in the rock he was excavating. The gunpowder exploded prematurely, launching it up into his left cheek and out of his head, landing like a javelin 25 yards away. Miraculously, he survived the injury, but he was not the same person; his personality had changed. Instead of the quiet, unassuming individual he had been before, his behaviour was characterised by rudeness and irresponsibility. The accident had destroyed his frontal lobe, the part of the brain involved in decision making, social behaviour and impulse control.

Over a century later, we still describe people as 'frontal' if they become less shy or 'disinhibited' by damage to this critical part of the brain. Frontal lobe disinhibition is relatively common, but rarer brain conditions can give us even more intriguing insights. For example, some people suddenly lose the ability to read, even though their vision remains functioning. They can even write normally, but bizarrely cannot read the words they have just written. This is a condition, known as 'alexia without agraphia'. It occurs when a stroke, (a blockage in blood supply), damages the *corpus callosum*, a collection of neurons that connect the two halves of the brain. Therefore, although in these instances they could see the words and process the images, the brain could not

send this information to the language areas on the left side of the brain where it is interpreted.

During Brain Awareness Week, it might be a good time to stop and think about your brain, if you rarely do. The week, celebrated annually in March, is an international campaign started in 1995 to raise awareness of the progress and benefits of brain research. Over the last 20 years, there have been some remarkable developments. We have created completely new drugs to treat patients with strokes and our ability to treat infections of the brain, including meningitis, has also come on in leaps and bounds. However, we have barely had an impact on dementia, a brain disease where neurons just wither away and die. We still do not understand the basic triggers for this brain condition.

Terry Pratchett, the well-known fantasy fiction writer, spent the last few years of his life thinking a lot about his brain and its shrinking cortex. He even tried an experimental light treatment to slow the decay. Another writer, Roald Dahl was fascinated by the impact of disease on the brain. He had the unique claim of helping neurosurgeon Kenneth Till and hydraulic engineer Stanley Wade develop a device known as the 'Wade-Dahl-Till' or WDT. This valve, designed to drain excess fluid from the head, was successfully used to treat his four-year-old son's hydrocephalus, or water on the brain; a condition that can leave patients with enormously swollen heads due to the accumulation of fluid in the skull. The youngster had previously been fitted with a device called a 'Pudenz', but it kept jamming. The device Dahl worked on subsequently helped thousands of people around the world suffering from the same rare medical condition.

You may not have Pratchett's creative talents or Dahl's sheer ingenuity, but spend a little time this week alone with your brain. Let it know that you cherish its extraordinary abilities and give it the respect it deserves.

Read the questions but don't worry about doing this exercise yet.

Questions 1–9

Answer the questions. Choose NO MORE THAN THREE WORDS from the passage for each answer.

1 Which organ of the body commands more of people's attention than the brain, according to the passage?
2 What can the texture of the brain be compared to?
3 What place does the arrangement of neurons in the brain resemble?
4 Which object penetrated Gage's face resulting in injury?
5 Which two personality traits did Gage display after his accident?
6 Which sense remains unaffected by the brain condition *alexia without agraphia*?
7 Which brain condition has seen little progress in treatments in the last 20 years?
8 What is the name of the author who contributed to the invention of a medical device?
9 What prevented the 'Pudenz' from working effectively?

1a **How much do you know about the human brain? Do the quiz.**

1 How much does the human brain weigh?
  A 0.5 kilos ☐   B 1.3 kilos ☐

2 What colour is the brain?
  A grey ☐   B pink ☐

3 How many nerve cells does the brain contain?
  A 100 billion ☐   B 300 billion ☐

4 What part of the brain is involved in decision making?
  A the frontal lobe ☐   B the *corpus callosum* ☐

5 On which side of the brain is language processed?
  A the right ☐   B the left ☐

6 What is the purpose of Brain Awareness Week?
  A to fund brain research ☐   B to inform people about brain research ☐

7 When was Brain Awareness Week established?
  A in the 1980s ☐   B in the 1990s ☐

1b **Read the text quickly and check your guesses. The answers follow the order of the text.**

2 **Underline the question word and key words in the first FOUR questions of the text. Then decide what kind of word you need to look for in the text.**

 **Get it right!**

Read the questions and the student's answers. What is wrong with the answers? Match the answers with the advice (a–d) below.

Choose **NO MORE THAN THREE WORDS** from the passage for each answer.

Question 1: Which organ of the body commands more of our attention than the brain, according to the passage?

Answer 1: haert

a Don't write more than the number of words you are asked for. You mustn't write full sentences.

....

Question 2: What can the texture of the brain be compared to?

Answer 2: It can be compared to a mushroom.

b Make sure you use the correct information when you answer a question.

....

Question 3: What place does the arrangement of neurons in the brain resemble?

Answer 3: Neurotransmitter signals

c Don't change words in the text. Remember the instructions tell you to choose words from the text.

....

Question 4: Which object penetrated Gage's face, resulting in injury?

Answer 4: an iron bar

d Be careful with spelling. You will lose marks if your spelling is wrong.

....

Correct the student's answers. Compare your suggestions with a partner.

Follow the same procedure as Exercise 2 to answer Questions 5–9.

5 Which two personality traits did Gage display after his accident?

....

6 Which sense remains unaffected by the brain condition *alexia without agraphia*?

....

7 Which brain condition has seen little progress in treatments in the last 20 years?

....

8 What is the name of the author who contributed to the invention of a medical device?

....

9 What prevented the 'Pudenz' from working effectively?

....

3 Read the questions but don't worry about doing this exercise yet.

William Henry Perkin

Perkin pioneered synthetic purple dye, changing the history of clothing.

Historically textile dyes were made from such natural sources as plants and animal excretions. Some of these, such as the glandular mucus of snails, were difficult to obtain and outrageously expensive. The colour purple, for example, extracted from a snail, was once so costly that in society at the time only the rich could afford it. Further, natural dyes tended to be muddy in hue and fade quickly. It was against this backdrop that Perkin's discovery was made.

Perkin quickly grasped that his purple solution could be used to colour fabric, thus making it the world's first synthetic dye. Realising the importance of this breakthrough, he lost no time in patenting it. But perhaps the most fascinating of all Perkin's reactions to his find was his nearly instant recognition that the new dye had commercial possibilities.

Perkin originally named his dye Tyrian purple, but it later became commonly known as mauve – from the French for the plant used to make the colour violet. He asked the advice of Scottish dye works owner Robert Pullar, who assured him that manufacturing the dye would be well worth it if the colour remained fast (i.e. would not fade) and the cost was relatively low.

With the help of his father and brother, Perkin set up a factory not far from London. Utilising the cheap and plentiful coal tar that was an almost unlimited by-product of London's gas street lighting, the dye works began producing the world's first synthetically dyed material in 1857. The company received a commercial boost from the Empress Eugenie of France when she decided the new colour flattered her. Very soon, mauve was the necessary shade for all the fashionable ladies in that country. Not to be outdone, England's Queen Victoria also appeared in public wearing a mauve gown, thus making it all the rage in England as well. The dye was bold and fast, and the public clamoured for more. Perkin went back to the drawing board.

Although Perkin's fame was achieved and fortune assured by his first discovery, the chemist continued his research. Among other dyes he developed and introduced were aniline red (1859) and aniline black (1863) and, in the late 1860s, Perkin's green. It is important to note that Perkin's synthetic dye discoveries had outcomes far beyond the merely decorative. The dyes also became vital to medical research in many ways. For instance, they were used to stain previously invisible microbes and bacteria, allowing researchers to identify such bacilli as tuberculosis, cholera and anthrax. Artificial dyes continue to play a crucial role today. And, in what would have been particularly pleasing to Perkin, their current use is in the search for a vaccine against malaria.

Answer the questions below. Choose NO MORE THAN TWO WORDS from the passage for each answer.

1 Before Perkin's discovery, with what group in society was the colour purple associated?

....

2 What potential did Perkin immediately understand that his new dye had? ....

3 What was the name finally used to refer to the first colour Perkin invented? ....

4 What was the name of the person Perkin consulted before setting up his own dye works?

....

5 In what country did Perkin's newly invented colour first become fashionable? ....

6 According to the passage, which disease is now being targeted by researchers using synthetic dyes?

....

Letter of complaint

1

2

3

4

1 ▶ **Match the extracts (A–C) with the pictures (1–4). There is one picture that you do not need to use.**

A | I am writing to complain about an online delivery I received yesterday. Not only did the package arrive two weeks later than expected, but the box was also in extremely bad condition. Fortunately, the camera it contained was undamaged, but the USB stick I had ordered was missing.

B | I am writing to make a complaint about the recent package holiday I had with *CityDreamz*. I had been promised a room with a river view, whereas, in fact, my window overlooked a tall block of flats, which made the room extremely dark. Furthermore, I had no tea-making facilities in the room, although the website had clearly stated that these would be provided in every room.

C | To make matters worse, when I opened the package, the majority of the crockery items were broken. In light of these issues, I would therefore like to request a full refund on the cost of the tea set together with the additional delivery charges paid.

2 Look again at the extracts in Exercise 1. What best describes the style and tone of each one?

A formal ☐ **B** informal ☐

3 Choose the most appropriate formal language for the following phrases from the text.

1 I am writing to complain about …
  A I want to say I'm not happy about … about … ☐
  B I am writing to express my dissatisfaction with … ☐

2 I had been promised …
  A You said I'd get … ☐
  B I had expected … ☐

3 To make matters worse …
  A Even more worrying is the fact that … ☐
  B If that wasn't bad enough … ☐

4 I would like to request a refund …
  A I want my money back. ☐
  B I would be grateful if you could reimburse me with the full amount. ☐

5 item
  A product ☐
  B something ☐

6 issues
  A things ☐
  B problems ☐

4 Read the extracts again and (circle) either YES or NO to complete the checklist for writing a good formal letter. Underline examples in the extracts A–C.

Formal letters …

1	have an impersonal formal tone.	YES	NO
2	contain simpler words ('got' instead of 'received').	YES	NO
3	may contain more passive forms.	YES	NO
4	contain contractions throughout.	YES	NO

5 Read the task and underline the three things you need to write about.

> *You recently booked a short holiday with a company called CitiDreamz and stayed in a hotel. You were not happy with your accommodation. You contacted the reception staff, but you were unsatisfied with their response.*
>
> *Write a letter to the manager of CitiDreamz. In your letter*
> * *describe the problem with the accommodation*
> * *explain what happened when you contacted reception staff*
> * *say what you would like the manager to do*
>
> *Write at least 150 words. You do NOT need to write any addresses.*

6 **Make notes for each of the prompts. There is a suggestion to help you.**

My room was very small!

7a **Read one part of the student's letter. Which prompt in the question are they writing about? 1, 2 or 3?** ....

> You promised me / I was promised a hotel in a central location, whereas in fact / but the hotel was far away / was located a long distance from the city centre. And another thing was / to make matters worse, the central heating did not work and so the room was very cold – particularly at night. I had been looking forward to this holiday very much, but it was completely ruined by these issues / things.

7b **Read the student's letter again. (Circle) the most appropriate underlined phrases for a letter of complaint.**

◉ Get it right!

Look at the following sentences taken from letters of complaint. There is a word missing in each one. Add the missing words to the sentences.

1 I am writing to complain my recent stay in your hotel.

....

2 I had promised a room with a view of the river.

....

3 I had been looking forward this holiday very much.

....

4 My holiday was completely ruined these issues.

....

5 I would be grateful you could refund half the cost of my holiday.

....

---

8 Write your own answer for the task in Exercise 5. When you have finished, compare it to the checklist in Exercise 5.

....
....
....
....
....
....
....
....
....
....
....
....
....
....
....
....
....
....
....
....

Compare your letter to the suggested answer given in the key.

 **Test task**

9 Now do the test practice task. Read the text in the box and write your answer.

> *You recently bought a piece of equipment for your kitchen, but it did not work. You phoned the shop to try to resolve the matter, but you remain unhappy with the situation.*
>
> *Write a letter to the shop manager. In your letter*
> - *describe the problem with the equipment*
> - *explain what happened when you phoned the shop*
> - *say what you would like the manager to do*

Write at least 150 words.

You do NOT need to write any addresses.

....
....
....
....
....
....
....
....
....
....
....
....
....
....
....
....
....
....
....
....

Job application

1  2  3

1 ▸ **Match the job advertisements (A–C) with the pictures (1–3).**

A

Olive Tree Hotel

- Are you a 'people' person?
- Are you willing to start work early and finish late?
- Have you got experience in the catering industry?

If you can answer 'yes' to all three questions, write to the manager, explaining why you are suitable to be a waiter in our busy hotel restaurant and enclosing a copy of your CV.

B

Tourist Guides needed

If you are knowledgeable about this beautiful, historic city and have excellent communication skills, then we want to hear from you! Write a letter to Mr Jackson, saying why you would like to join our growing team of tourist guides this summer!

C

Camp Leader wanted!

We are looking for people to help lead our various activity camps in July and August. You will keep kids busy and entertained outdoors in the summer sunshine. Interested? Then send your application to Ms Akhtar, stating why you would be ideal for the role.

2 ▶ **Read the advertisements again. For which job do the following statements apply? Write the correct letter (A–C). You may have to write more than one letter for some of the statements.**

For which job(s)

1 do you need to work with children? ....

2 do you have to work long hours? ....

3 are you expected to have previous relevant experience? ....

4 can you close your letter with 'Yours sincerely'? ....

5 must you start your letter with 'Dear Sir or Madam'? ....

3 ▶ **Read the following task. Then answer the questions. Do not write your answer yet.**

> *You have seen an advertisement for reception staff and waiting staff in a hotel in July and August.*
>
> *Write a letter to the hotel manager. In your letter*
> - *say which job you would like to do*
> - *explain why you would be suitable for the job*
> - *offer availability for one or both months*
>
> **Write at least 150 words. You do NOT need to write any addresses.**
>
> **Begin your letter as follows:**
>
> *Dear Sir or Madam,*

1 What kind of letter do you need to write?

    A formal ☐   **B** formal ☐

    <u>Underline</u> the three things in the question that you need to do.

2 Which job in the hotel would YOU choose to apply for – receptionist or waiter? Make notes for the three prompts below.

....

....

....

4 Read the pairs of phrases and sentences. Which is the most suitable to include in a job application, A or B?

1 **A** I would like to get a job in your hotel. ☐

   B I am writing to apply for a job in your hotel. ☐

2 **A** I would be interested in this job opportunity because … ☐

   B I would love the job because … ☐

3 **A** Please will you … ☐

   B I would be grateful if you would … ☐

4 **A** Write soon! ☐

   B I look forward to hearing from you. ☐

5 **A** Yours faithfully ☐

   B Cheers ☐

5a Read part of the student's answer which got a band score of 4.5. Answer the questions.

> I would discribe myself as friendly and hard-working. I also working well as part of a team. i understand that on a hotel, customer satissfaction are extremely important so I know I need to be familliar with all the dishes in the menu before I takes orders for lunch or dinner.

1 Which job does the student choose to apply for? ....

2 Which part of the question are they writing about – 1, 2 or 3? ....

✓ **Test tips**

It is important to proofread your work very carefully, checking for spelling, punctuation and grammatical errors.

5b Read the student's answer again. Find and correct the following errors.

1 THREE spelling mistakes

2 THREE errors in verb forms

3 TWO incorrect uses of prepositions

4 ONE error with capital letters

6 ▶ Write your own answer to the task in Exercise 3. Use the phrases in Exercise 4 to help you.

....
....
....
....
....
....
....
....
....
....
....
....
....
....
....
....

Read your completed answer and answer the questions.

- Have you included all THREE points from the task?   ☐
- Have you used a formal style for opening and closing your letter?   ☐
- Have you proofread your work for errors in spelling, punctuation and grammar?   ☐

Compare your answer to the one given in the key.

 **Test task**

7 Now do the test practice task. Read the text in the box and write your answer.

> *You have seen an advertisement for the job of instructor at a children's activity camp in the summer holidays. Instructors need to be able to teach two sports.*
>
> *Write a letter to the activity camps manager. In your letter*
> - *explain why you would be suitable for the job of instructor*
> - *say which sporting activities you would like to teach and why*
> - *offer to work for one or more months of the summer holidays*

Write at least 150 words. You do NOT need to write any addresses.

Begin your letter as follows:

Dear Sir or Madam,

....

....

....

....

....

....

....

....

....

....

....

....

....

....

....

....

....

....

....

....

....

A personal letter

1a **Read extracts A and B from letters as quickly as you can.**

A

Great news! I'm writing to let you know that at last we've moved house! We just couldn't go on living in the two-bedroom flat now that the twins are growing up and the new baby's arrived. We've got three bedrooms now, and there's a very modern bathroom and a spacious kitchen too. So, would you like to come round for dinner on Saturday evening – say 7pm? Let me know if that's good for you. Can't wait to find out what you think of our new place!

B

<u>I'm really sorry but</u> I won't be able to pick you up from the station on Friday. My car broke down yesterday and I've had to take it to the garage for repair and it won't be ready for me to collect until next week. I'm not at all happy that it's going to take as long as that to get fixed. What a pain! So it'd be best to take the number 43 bus into the city centre. I'll meet you there instead. Then, how about we find a nice café where we can sit down and have something to eat? Let me know what you think.

1b **What best describes the style and tone of the letters?**

formal ☐   informal ☐

2 Read the short extracts again and write the correct letter A or B. For one of the questions you have to write both letters.

In which extract, A or B, or both, is someone

1 describing?   ....
2 suggesting?   ....
3 inviting?   ....
4 explaining why something has happened?   ....
5 apologising?   ....
6 advising?   ....
7 complaining?   ....

3 <u>Underline</u> the phrases in the extracts that are used to convey the different actions in Exercise 2. There is an example to help you.

I'm really sorry but ...... – apologising

4 Read the extracts again and (circle) either YES or NO to complete the checklist for writing a good informal letter. <u>Underline</u> examples in the extracts A and B.

Personal letters …

1 have a friendly, informal tone   YES   NO
2 can include exclamation marks   YES   NO
3 use full forms (I will, does not)   YES   NO
4 can include incomplete sentences   YES   NO
5 include phrasal verbs   YES   NO

5a Read the task and <u>underline</u> the three things you have to do in your letter.

> *You have recently moved to a new city.*
>
> *Write a letter to an English-speaking friend. In your letter*
>
> • *explain why you have moved*
> • *describe the new city*
> • *invite your friend to come and visit*
>
> **Write at least 150 words. You do NOT need to write any addresses.**

5b Make notes for each of the prompts in the question. Look at the student's idea to help you.

I've got a new job! ....

....

....

6a Read one part of the student's letter. Which prompt in the question are they writing about? 1, 2 or 3?

> Leeds really is a lively city – you would love it here! It is a university city so there are always lots of young people around. There is always something new and exciting to do. Great fun! I have come across some amazing music venues where there are some live bands at weekends. My flat looks out over a lovely park and it is a great place to go jogging or have a picnic – especially when the weather is good.

....

6b Read the student's letter again. Compare it to the checklist in Exercise 4. Which advice do they NOT follow?

....
....

6c Rewrite the paragraph. Make the changes to follow all the advice and then compare with a partner.

....
....
....
....
....

7 Write your own answer for the task in Exercise 5a. When you have finished, complete the checklist in Exercise 4.

....
....
....
....
....
....
....
....
....
....
....
....
....

Compare your letter to the one in the answer key.

 **Test facts**

Writing Part 1

In Writing Part 1 you may have to write a formal or an informal letter. You may be asked to write a formal letter to a manager of a shop, for example, or you may have to write an informal letter to an English-speaking friend.

For both types of letter, you have to show that you can use language for a range of different functions. For example, you may have to apologise or complain about something or perhaps ask for information or give a description. The question will always give you clear instructions about which actions you need to use in your letter.

 **Test task**

8 ▸ **Now do the test practice task.**

> *You have recently moved to new accommodation. Write a letter to an English-speaking friend. In your letter*
> - *explain why you have moved*
> - *describe the new accommodation*
> - *invite your friend to come and visit*

Write at least 150 words. You do NOT need to write any addresses.

Begin your letter as follows:

Dear ...

....
....
....
....
....
....
....
....
....
....
....
....
....

Discussion essay

1a **Read the descriptions of three unusual museums and match them to the pictures. Ignore the gaps for now.**

A   B   C

1 The instant noodles museum in Osaka, Japan features **a** .... that give information about the history of instant noodles. The museum even has a special tunnel that visitors can walk through to see packages of instant noodles from all over the world. You can also play some **b** .... games, one of which includes designing packaging for your own cup of noodles to take away as a **c** .... of your visit.

2 Leila's hair museum in Missouri, USA has a **d** .... of more than 2,000 pieces of **e** .... made from human hair. These include rings, necklaces and earrings. There are also samples of hair from famous people **f** ....

3 The Cancun Underwater Museum in Mexico can be found deep in the Caribbean Sea so it is only **g** .... to certified divers. There are more than 500 **h** .... human figures, vehicles and buildings. Each **i** .... is made from special concrete that helps coral and algae to grow around it. The aim of the museum is to highlight the importance of **j** .... marine life.

1b **Complete the descriptions of the museums with the words in the box.**

accessible	collection	exhibits	interactive	jewellery
life-size	on display	preserving	sculpture	souvenir

2a **Read the following task.**

In many countries, people have to pay an admission fee to enter museums. Some people believe that it is reasonable for museums to charge admission fees. Others believe that entry to museums should be free of charge.

Discuss both these views and give your own opinion.

Write at least 250 words.

2b **What do you have to do? Tick (✓) A or B?**

A Select one of the views to focus on and explain why you agree. ☐

B Make some notes about the two views and give your own view. ☐

3 ▸ Make notes for the task in Exercise 2 below. There is an example to help you.

First view: *museums need money to pay their staff*

....

Second view: ....

....

My view: ....

....

4a ▸ Look at the points the student has made about admission fees for museums. Do they mention any of your ideas?

1 <u>There is no doubt that</u> museums are expensive places to run. ....

2 <u>It is important to take into account that</u> some people live far from museums so they have travel costs to consider as well. ....

3 <u>It is impossible to argue with the fact that</u> museums need to keep acquiring new exhibits. ....

4 <u>Some people think that</u> charges could deter poorer people from visiting. ....

5 <u>It is important to remember that</u> people already pay for other entertainment and leisure activities. ....

4b ▸ Which of the points could be used to support the first view and which could be used to support the second view? Put 1 or 2 next to each one.

5 ▸ Look at the <u>underlined</u> phrases in Exercise 4a. Most of them can be used to introduce the views you agree with. Which ONE phrase can be used to introduce views of people you don't agree with? ....

6b ▸ Look back at the notes you made in Exercise 3. Write sentences saying why you agree or disagree with each point you made.

....

....

....

....

....

☑ **Test tips**

In order to write a well-developed argument, you need to include main points and information which supports each point.

7 Match the student's points 1–5 in Exercise 4a with the supporting information A–E below. Write 1–5 at the end of each statement.

Supporting information

A They have to buy tickets to watch films at the cinema or enjoy performances at the theatre, for example. ....

B It is important for them to attract visitors by adding paintings, sculptures and manuscripts to their collections. ....

C As well as those on low incomes, large families and school groups may also be unable to afford to go to museums if they are expected to pay. ....

D Some visitors may have to travel very long distances in order to visit a museum. They may be deterred from doing so if they have to pay an admission charge in addition to the cost of their journey. ....

E In order to operate at all, museums need revenue so that they can pay the salaries of their staff. Their employees include guides and specialist curators who help to preserve the exhibits. ....

8a Read Paragraphs 2 and 3 of the student's answer below. Ignore the gaps for now.

1 .... admission charges may prevent large families from going to museums. However, many museums already offer discounts for big groups and young children are admitted free of charge. Furthermore, there are museums that allow free entry on one day of each week. For example, in my city, they are free for visitors every Monday.

2 .... museums are far from cheap places to run. They have to pay their staff as well as meet the costs of heating, lighting and security. It seems reasonable that visitors who enjoy looking at the exhibits on display should contribute to these expenses.

3 .... people pay to enjoy many other leisure activities like going to football matches and concerts. Surely, they should be prepared to pay to enter a museum as well.

4 .... museums need to stay relevant and continue to appeal to a wide range of people and age groups. In order to do this, they need to invest in fun, educational interactive displays and facilities like cafes and shops. Without revenue generated by admission fees, they will not be able to keep the museum up to date and interesting.

8b Answer the questions.

1 Which view does the writer agree with in the task – the first view or the second view?

....

....

2 Which ideas in Exercise 4a does the writer mention?

....

....

3 Does the writer consider the other view?

....

....

4 Does the writer give an example from their own experience?

....

....

8c **Complete the gaps in the text with the phrases (A–D).**

A Furthermore, it is impossible to argue against the fact that

B However, there is no doubt that

C Finally, it is important to remember that

D Some people argue that

9 **Write your own Paragraphs 2 and 3. Use the phrases in Exercise 8c to help you structure your answer. You can use some of the ideas in Exercise 4a to help you.**

....

....

....

....

....

....

....

....

10a **Look at the two plans (A and B) for writing an introduction and a conclusion.**

A	B
Paragraph 1 (Introduction)	Paragraph 1 (Introduction)
Opinion	General introduction (no opinion)
Paragraph 4 (conclusion)	Paragraph 4 (Conclusion)
Restate opinion	Opinion given for the first time

10b **Read the student's paragraphs. Which plan does the student follow? A or B?**

Paragraph 1

Many people enjoy visiting museums in their leisure time to admire the amazing exhibits on display – from dinosaur bones to unusual sculptures. Some people take the view that museums should be free to all visitors, while others think that it is fair for museums to impose an entry fee. I firmly believe that admission charges are a good thing. ....

Paragraph 4

All in all, I strongly believe that it is fair for museums to charge people for admission. These important centres of learning play a valuable part in preserving our history and need revenue from visitors to keep their collections exciting and accessible to all. ....

11 **Choose ONE of the plans (A or B) in Exercise 10a to follow. Write your own introduction and conclusion.**

....
....
....
....
....
....
....
....
....
....

12 Now do the test practice task. Present a written argument or case to an educated reader with no specialist knowledge on the following topic.

> *Some people believe that trips to places such as museums and art galleries should be a compulsory part of high school programmes. Others say that students should complete all their learning within the classroom.*
>
> *Discuss both these views and give your own opinion.*

Give reasons for your answer and include any relevant examples from your own knowledge or experience. Write at least 250 words.

....
....
....
....
....
....
....
....
....
....
....
....
....
....
....
....
....
....
....
....
....
....
....

Double question essay

1 ▶ **Read the following task.**

> *Nowadays more and more people are taking short flights to places in their own country, which causes environmental problems. Some people say that the government should impose a higher tax on these flights.*
> *Do you think a higher tax on short flights is a good idea?*
> *In what other ways might the environmental problems caused by these flights be reduced?*
>
> Give reasons for your answer and include any relevant examples from your own knowledge or experience.
>
> Write at least 250 words.

What idea are you being asked to agree or disagree with? ....

....

2 ▶ **Do the quiz. Match the definitions on the topic of the environment with the phrases in the box.**

Environment Word Quiz

Definitions

1 This describes residents taking holidays within their own country, for example, Britons who holiday in Cornwall. ....

2 This means the same as renewable energy, which comes from natural resources rather than non-renewable sources. These sources cause less harm to the natural environment.

....

3 This involves having as little impact as possible on the environment when making a journey. For example, this may involve choosing to travel by rail instead of air. ....

4 This describes toxic substances, for example, harmful gases or chemicals deposited into the atmosphere. They can have a severe negative impact on the local environment, and in large quantities, on a global scale. ....

5 This refers to policies, laws, services or products that have a minimal or reduced impact on the environment. ....

6 This is a type of fuel used in trains, buses and other vehicles...

7 This is the increase in world temperatures caused by polluting gas. ....

8 This involves buying carbon credits, giving money to help fund projects such as planting trees or investing in renewable energy. These projects aim to reduce the amount of carbon emissions by a measurable amount. ....

9 This describes the large amount of greenhouse gas (including carbon dioxide and methane) which is generated by human activities. Ways of reducing this include using public transport and consuming food that doesn't require much transportation. ....

air pollution	diesel fuel	domestic tourism	eco-friendly	global warming
green energy	large carbon footprint	offsetting your emissions	sustainable travel	

3 Look at the words and phrases in Exercise 2 again. Group them under the two headings below. There is an example to help you.

Good for the environment	Bad for the environment
	diesel

4a Read the student's introduction to the first question in the task.

> There is no doubt that more and more travellers are choosing to take domestic flights these days which is seriously affecting the environment. This is because individual short trips can have a remarkably large carbon footprint. However, despite the high carbon emissions produced by planes, I firmly believe that tackling the problem of global warming needs far more than a simple tax to make people reconsider how they travel.

4b What best describes their view?

A strong agreement ☐ **B** partial agreement ☐ **C** strong disagreement ☐

5 Look at the points below. Which points support agreement and which support disagreement? Put A for Agreement or D for Disagreement next to each one.

1 Trains produce fewer carbon emissions than planes. ....

2 Taxing flights would be especially unfair for people who live in a remote area ... .

3 The taxes could provide extra revenue for the government ... .

4 Higher taxes might provide an incentive for airlines to produce more fuel-efficient planes ... .

5 It is not right to limit people's personal freedom to travel in the way they want. ....

6 ➤ **Match the points 1–5 in Exercise 5 with the endings A–E below. Write 1–5 at the end of each statement.**

A … <u>but</u> this money would not necessarily be used to tackle the very serious problem of air pollution. ....

B <u>Nevertheless</u>, I do understand those who say that restricting an individual's freedom of choice is a small price to pay and that immediate action is needed. ....

C <u>However</u>, it is important to remember that they are not a source of clean energy either. ....

D … <u>although</u> there is likely to be resistance from some companies. ....

E … <u>despite</u> the seriousness of the problem of emissions caused by internal flights within a country. ....

7 ➤ **Write the correct linking words from Exercise 6 in the spaces below to complete the rules.**

1 _____

It can be used to introduce a contrasting idea.

It can go at the beginning of a sentence or in the middle.

It is followed by a noun.

2 _____ _____

It is used to contrast two ideas in the same sentence.

It can go at the beginning of a sentence or in the middle.

If it goes at the beginning of a sentence, there is a comma in the middle.

3 _____

It is used to contrast two ideas in the same sentence.

It goes in the middle of the sentence.

4 _____ _____

It is used to contrast ideas in two different sentences.

It usually goes at the beginning of the second sentence.

It is immediately followed by a comma.

 **Get it right!**

Read the student's sentences. Correct them by using different linking words.

1 Despite fewer flights would mean more trains, this could place pressure on the rail network.

2 Travelling by rail or bus may take longer than flying however you get to see more of the country than you would by sitting on a plane.

8 Which of the points in Exercise 5 do you agree and disagree with? Can you add your own ideas? Make notes below.

....

....

....

....

....

9a Read part of the student's answer to the task. Ignore the <u>underlined</u> words for now. Which of the main ideas in Exercise 5 and YOUR ideas do they mention?

> There is no doubt that an increasing number of people are choosing to take domestic flights these days and this is having a serious impact on the environment. This is because these individual short trips can have a remarkably large carbon footprint. However, <u>despite / although</u> the high carbon emissions produced by planes, I strongly believe that tackling the problem of global warming is likely to need more than a simple tax.
>
> <u>Although / Despite</u> there can be no doubt that short flights are a huge source of carbon emissions, imposing a tax is unlikely to discourage people from flying short distances – particularly those who live in remote areas and have no other option but to fly. In my country, for example, people have no choice <u>however / but</u> to travel from islands to the mainland by air because the journey by boat takes too much time. Furthermore, it is sometimes the case that it is cheaper to fly than to use other forms of transport such as the train or the car. <u>Nevertheless / Although</u>, there are various other measures that could be implemented to reduce carbon emissions.

....

9b Choose the correct <u>underlined</u> linking words to complete the candidate's answer. You can look back at the rules for the use of linking words in Exercise 7.

10 Look again at the second question in the task: 'What other measures do you think would be effective?' Make notes about your ideas. There is an example to help you.

<u>Build more railway tracks so that people can travel by train instead.</u>..................................

....

....

....

....

11 Read the student's answer to the second question in the task. Which THREE measures do they suggest? Are any of your ideas mentioned?

> Nevertheless, there are various other measures that could be implemented that would have a huge effect on reducing greenhouse gas emissions. Firstly, governments could persuade airlines to design planes which have more efficient engines and use cleaner fuels. Furthermore, there needs to be more investment in improving bus and rail services and ensuring that these run efficiently and that the infrastructure is maintained. This would make people far more willing to consider travelling between cities by bus or train. Finally, I think that there is a need for more education about the effects of global warming and how cutting back on air travel could have a positive impact. For example, some people simply do not realise just how polluting short flights are.

....

....

....

12a Write your own answer to the task. When you have finished, complete the checklist below.

....

....

....

....

....

....

....

....

....

....

....

....

....

....

....

....

....

Have you …

- given your opinion in the first paragraph? ☐
- considered both sides of the argument? ☐
- used examples to support your points? ☐
- included some linking expressions? ☐
- answered the second question? ☐
- restated your opinion in the final paragraph? ☐

12b **Compare your answer to the suggested answer in the key.**

☑ **Test task**

13 **Now do the test practice task. Read the text in the box and write your answer.**

> *Some people say that increasing the price of petrol (gas) is the best way to solve traffic and pollution problems in towns and cities.*
>
> *Do you agree or disagree?*
>
> *In what other ways could these problems be solved?*

Give reasons for your answer and include any relevant examples from your own knowledge or experience. Write at least 250 words.

....
....
....
....
....
....
....
....
....
....
....
....
....
....
....

Friends and family

1 🔊 **Track 31 Complete the questions (1–4) with the words in the box. Listen and check your answers, then discuss the questions in pairs.**

alike	like	like doing	look like

1 Are you and your friends ....?

2 What are your family ....?

3 What do you and your friends .... together?

4 Who, in your family, do you .... most?

2 🔊 **Track 32 Match the questions (1–4) from Exercise 1 to the appropriate answers (A–D). Then listen and check your answers.**

A It depends on the weather really. If it's nice, we love chilling out in the park. It helps us relax after a hard day at college.

B Well, mum's tall and elegant and quite strict – especially about things like keeping my room tidy, or when I want to stay out late with my mates.

C That'll be my dad. Our features are very similar; for example, we've got the same chin and nose.

D I'm like my best friend Martha. We're both quite impatient and when it comes to sports, we're very competitive as we hate losing.

3 **Put a cross next to the things you should NOT say if you don't hear the examiner when they ask you a question.**

1 What? ☐

2 Pardon? ☐

3 Sorry? ☐

4 Repeat? ☐

4 🔊 **Track 33 Put the words into the correct order to complete a suitable two-sentence response when you don't hear what the examiner has said. The first sentence has been done for you. Then listen and check your answers.**

1 please you could again it say
'I didn't quite catch that....................... . Could you say it again please.................?'

2 question repeat you could the
'Sorry, I missed that....................... . ...?'

3 mind you saying again that would please
'I couldn't quite hear you....................... . ...?'

5 🔊 **Track 34 Listen to four students answering Part 1 questions. Decide which statement (1–4) applies to which candidate (A–D).**

1 The student's answer is too short and the examiner needs to ask a follow-up question. ....

2 The student's answer is too long and goes off topic. ....

3 The student's answer is clearly a prepared speech. ....

4 The student's answer is full and sounds natural. ....

6 ▸ **Put the words and phrases into the correct columns.**

as	due to	for instance	including	like
since		such as	this happens because	

Words and phrases to give examples	Words and phrases to give reasons

7 ▸ **Think about how you would answer these questions. Then match the questions to the answer pairs (A–G).**

1 Do you often go out with your family at the weekends? (Why/Why not?)

2 Have you always liked the same type of family holidays? (Why/Why not?)

3 Would you like to move, with your family, to another town or city? (Why/Why not?)

4 Are there any sports you dislike playing? (Why/Why not?)

5 Is there anything you did with your family in the past, that you don't do now? (Why/Why not?)

6 Did you enjoy making friends when you first started school? (Why/Why not?)

7 Was there anything you disliked about school? (Why/Why not?)

A No, there isn't. / Yes, there is.

B No, I don't. / Yes, I do.

C No, I wouldn't. / Yes, I would.

D No, I didn't. / Yes, I did

E No, I haven't. / Yes, I have.

F No, there wasn't. / Yes, there was.

G No, there aren't. / Yes, there are.

☑ Test task

8 🔊 **Track 35** **Listen to Laya answering the questions about sports fully and naturally. As you listen, make a note of the examples and reasons she gives. Also, which question does Laya not completely answer?**

1 Do you enjoy playing sports?

2 Is there any sport you would like to try in the future?

3 Do you often watch sport on TV?

4 What sports do children normally do at school in your country?

Notes

....
....
....
....
....
....
....
....

9 **Answer the questions in Exercise 8 yourself. Give full answers which include reasons and examples. If possible, record yourself answering the questions. Listen to your recording and check your answers against the questions (1–6) below. If you cannot record yourself, consider asking a friend to listen to you.**

1 Did I use suitable words or phrases to give examples? ☐

2 Did I use suitable words or phrases to give reasons? ☐

3 Did I give full answers? ☐

4 Were my answers too short? ☐

5 Were my answers too long? ☐

6 Did I move away from the topic? ☐

☑ Test facts

Worksheet 1 provides practice for Part 1 of the Speaking test. Part 1 will last about five minutes. The examiner will ask you questions about yourself and about other familiar topics, such as your family, your hometown or your likes and dislikes.

☑ Test tips

- You will not be penalised if you ask the examiner to repeat the question, as long as you don't keep doing it; however, make sure you know the correct way to ask them to repeat something.

- In Part 1 of the Speaking test, it is important to answer the examiner's questions fully and naturally. This means you should support yes/no answers with a reason or an example and avoid giving answers you have learnt from a prepared speech.

Descriptions

1 🔊 **Track 36 Listen to two students called Changying and Abbas talking about Part 2 of the IELTS Speaking test and answer the questions. You can listen more than once.**

1 What is Changying concerned about?

   A speaking without the examiner asking questions

   B speaking for up to two minutes

2 What revision strategy do Changying and Abbas disagree about?

   A Learning a wide range of grammar is as important as fluency.

   B Learning complete answers is useful.

3 How does Changying intend to improve her pronunciation?

   A by listening to native English speakers

   B by listening to examples of her own speaking practice

4 Why does Abbas think Changying should time herself speaking?

   A so she can practise speaking for the right amount of time

   B so she can check she's answered the question fully

5 Why does Changying agree it's better not to make up stories?

   A You will sound more confident.

   B You can give more details.

2 🔊 **Track 37 Look at the task and then listen to Changying giving her talk. As you listen, complete Changying's sentences (1–5).**

> **Describe a shop in your town or city that you sometimes use.**
>
> **You should say:**
>
>   **what sorts of products or service it sells**
>
>   **what type of people go there**
>
>   **where it is located**
>
> **and explain why you like going to this shop.**

1 You .... a local shop I go to every so often.

2 So, ..., I'm going to talk a shop called New From Old.

3 I think the .... go there are …

4 .... location, it's not far from where I live.

5 What .... why I like shopping in New From Old?

3 🔊 **Track 37** Changying uses linking language (e.g. *because of*, *due to*, *for example*) to expand her ideas, and pronouns and determiners (e.g. *she, he, they, it, that, this*) to avoid repetition. Listen again and put the phrases in the order you hear them. There is one you do not need.

A it's people like her who tend to go there ....

B but it's more than that ....

C like my Aunt Miriam, for example ....

D stuff like that ....

E so that's why I go there ....

F they repair it ....

G as I said ....

H when I say … I mean ....

4 Look at the task and the two sets of notes (A and B). Think about which style of notes you would be most comfortable using and why.

> Describe something you have seen that you would really like to own.
>   what the thing is
>   how long you have wanted to own it
>   where you first saw it
> and explain why you would like to own it.

A

How long have I wanted one?
• not entirely sure
• early childhood (around 5)

Where did I first see it?
bedtime story books

What *do* I want in the future?
a horse

Why *do* I want to own one?
• riding: takes skill and courage
• feelings: thrilling yet relaxing.
• fitness: time outdoors / fresh air

B

What: Video Game – New World

How long: Since it came out last year

Where: Can't quite remember. Could have been Akane's house / gaming competition

Why: Special effects / thrilling / all my mates have it

....

5 🔊 **Track 38 Listen to Abbas answering the question in Exercise 4. As you listen, write down the notes Abbas may have made before he started speaking. You can use any style of note taking you prefer, (e.g. a list, mind map or diagram).**

☑ Test task

6 Look at the task. Spend a minute making notes. Then use your notes to talk for one to two minutes. If you can, record yourself speaking so that you can listen after and think about how you can improve. If not, ask a friend to listen to you. Remember to use different points in the question to help you structure your talk and connect and expand your ideas with linking phrases and pronouns.

> **Describe someone you know who does something well.**
> **You should say:**
>   **who this person is**
>   **how you know them**
>   **what they do well**
> **and explain why you think this person is so good at doing this.**

☑ Test facts

In Speaking Part 2, you will be asked to talk about a specific topic. You will be given one minute to prepare before talking for between one and two minutes. You may be asked to describe a person, time, place or experience. You may also be asked to describe your feelings.

☑ Test tips

Two of the criteria that you are assessed on are coherence and fluency. Coherence means how well you organise your ideas so the listener can follow what you are saying. Using the different points in the task to structure your talk might help you to be more coherent.

Discussion topics

A

> should children ? which learn skills at school

B

> skills ? home should any are there at learn they which

C

> which be and important skills the future ? will in abilities

1 Put the words into the correct order to make questions. More than one option may be possible.

A .... ?

B .... ?

C .... ?

2 🔊 Track 39 Look at the techniques for developing ideas then listen to Berdine answering the questions in Exercise 1. Tick (✓) the techniques she uses.

Techniques for developing ideas

1 giving your own point of view or opinion ☐

2 giving others' points of view or ideas ☐

3 suggesting a solution to a problem ☐

4 explaining why something happens ☐

5 offering a contrasting idea ☐

6 making future predictions ☐

7 discussing advantages and/or disadvantages of something ☐

8 giving examples to support ideas ☐

9 giving factual information ☐

3 🔊 Track 39 Listen again and complete what Berdine says with the words you hear. You can listen more than once.

1 It .... that children …

2 One way .... this is to teach life skills.

3 Let's take socialising ....

4 .... they don't know how to properly socialise …

5 Well, ... that life skills …

6 For .... they may have no siblings …

7 .... I think children should learn …

8 I think we're .... skills related to that.

9 Technology offers us, and the planet, ... …

4 **Write the techniques from Exercise 2 next to the most appropriate phrases.**

1 some might suggest ....

2 the drawbacks are significant ....

3 things like that ....

4 one way of approaching this ....

5 as far as I'm concerned ....

6 it's unlikely that ....

7 as opposed to ....

8 it's a known fact that ....

9 this is due to ....

5 **Put the sentences into the correct categories in the table.**

1 That depends on the situation.

2 I'm not so sure about that.

3 I think we need to consider both sides.

4 My thoughts exactly.

5 That's not the way I see it.

6 There's no doubt about it.

Disagree	Neither disagree nor agree	Agree

6 🔊 **Track 40 In Part 3 Advik is asked about the topic of work and money. Look at one of the questions he was asked. Then, listen to Advik and answer the questions (1–3).**

EXAMINER: Some people say it would be better for society if everyone got the same salary. What do you think about that?

1 How far does Advik agree with the opinion in the question?

....

2 What phrase does he use to express his view?

....

3 What examples does he give to support his ideas?

....

....

....

....

✓ Test task

7 **Look at the questions and spend a minute deciding how you might answer them. Then answer the questions using the prompts to help you, if you wish. If possible, record yourself so you can listen afterwards and think about how you can improve. If not, ask a friend to listen to you and give you feedback. Remember to develop your ideas with reasons, examples, and solutions.**

Owning things

1 What types of things do young people in your country want to own nowadays?

2 Do you think television can make people want to own more things?

3 What should people do with things they no longer want?

4 Some people think owning things is a sign of success. Do you agree?

5 Would life be better if nobody owned private property?

Answer prompts:

Unlike in the past, …

As I see it …

One possibility might be to …

We could overcome this by …

I think we need to consider both sides …

It's highly likely that …

◉ Get it right!

If you are asked to give your opinion about the views of other people, or to talk about people generally, it is important that you do not talk only about yourself, friends or family as you did in Part 1. Look at the Part 3 question and then decide which is the best response (1–3).

EXAMINER: Do you think people will consider that having lots of possessions is a sign of success in the future?

RAJ (1): Well, I don't believe that having a lot of possessions will necessarily equal success in the future. For me, being successful will be about having a happy and healthy family rather than the number of items I own.

MARIA (2): Not really, no. I think the focus on having good mental health will continue and for many, success will be more about living a stress-free life, for example, less work and more family time, than buying flash cars.

HANU (3): Absolutely. My dad really wants to own a premium car, like a Lamborghini, in the future. He thinks it will show other people how successful he is. I'd like lots of expensive possessions in the future too.

 **Think about it** Listening Worksheet 1: Answering multiple-choice questions

Read the sentences and choose the correct options.

1 Questions will appear *in a random order / in the order you hear them*.

2 When answering questions *don't choose / choose* an option because it includes the same word you hear.

3 *Word matching / Listening for paraphrases* will usually help you select the correct option.

4 Look for options which express *the same idea / a different idea* as the speaker but in *the same way / a different way*.

5 You *will / won't* hear information about options other than the correct one.

6 *More than one / Only one* option will be correct for each question.

7 You will hear the Listening text *once / twice*.

8 Questions may focus on the ideas and opinions of the *speaker / listener*.

 **Think about it** Listening Worksheet 2: Answering matching questions

Read the statements. Are they TRUE or FALSE?

1 The speakers may contradict and correct each other. ....

2 Before you listen, it's a good idea to try to paraphrase the words in the options. ....

3 Paraphrases will not include opposites. For example, these opposites, *rather boring* instead of *not very interesting*. ....

4 Questions sometimes follow the order you hear them. ....

5 You know when questions are coming as they are clearly signposted in the text. ....

6 If you miss a question, spend time trying to answer it before moving on. ....

7 You will need to use all the options. ....

8 After listening, it's a good idea to use the remaining options to answer any questions you have missed. ....

Think about it ▸ Listening Worksheet 3: Flowchart completion

Match the sentence starters (1–8) with the endings (a–h) to make sentences about flowchart completion.

1 In flowchart completion, you must use a word or words from the Listening text	**a** ideas and move between topics.
2 Typically, the flowchart will show the order	**b** a question in each stage.
3 You may not need to answer	**c** needed for each gap.
4 Use the headings and subheadings on the question paper	**d** by connecting sentences with arrows.
5 Think about the type of word	**e** the order of the text you hear about them.
6 Signposting may be used to connect	**f** will not be the same as the words you hear.
7 The questions will follow	**g** to help you follow the speaker(s).
8 The words around the gap	**h** to complete the gaps.

Think about it ▸ Listening Worksheet 4: Labelling

Complete the sentences with the words from the box. Use each word once only.

compass	directions	letters	location	monologue	orientate	question	tourist

For map labelling, you will hear a **1** .... You may be asked to follow
2 .... so it's important to familiarise yourself with language of movement and
3 .... Maps may be of a part of a town or **4** .... destination.
As you listen, write down the correct letter next to the **5** .... The questions
follow the order of the Listening text and there may be **6** .... that you do not need
to use. If you are given a **7** .... icon, it is likely you will hear phrases like 'to the
east'. Use these phrases to help **8** .... yourself as you listen.

Think about it   Listening Worksheet 5: Table completion

Read the statements about table completion. Are they TRUE or FALSE?

1   Before you listen, you should use the headings to predict the type of word you need. ....

2   If the instructions say **write ONE word** and your answer contains TWO words, it might be correct. ....

3   If the answer is a plural noun form and you write down a singular noun form, you will not be penalised. ....

4   Asking yourself questions using the information either side of the gaps may develop your understanding and help you hear the correct answer. ....

5   Table-completion questions will only appear in Part 1 and Part 2 of the Listening test. ....

6   You may be asked to choose the correct answer from a number of options. ....

7   You should avoid making simple mistakes by reading the instructions carefully. ....

8   You should check your answers before transferring them to the answer sheet. ....

Think about it   Listening Worksheet 6: Note completion

Read the sentences and choose the correct options.

1   Before you listen, look at the questions and think about what paraphrases you *might hear / might not hear*.

2   Identifying synonyms and paraphrases will help you 'hear' when the *incorrect answer / correct answer* is coming.

3   Don't leave any question *answered / unanswered*.

4   *Guess / Don't guess* any answers you are not sure about.

5   You will need to listen for *specific / general* information.

6   Write down *a similar / the exact* word that you hear.

7   *Use / Don't use* the headings to help you follow the speaker.

8   The questions *follow / may not follow* the order of the text you hear about them.

Think about it ▸ Reading Worksheet 1: Matching statements

Complete the text about matching statements with the words from the box. Use each word once only.

beginning	jump	key	paraphrases	place	questions	statements	text

For this type of question, you are given a list of **1** .... which you need to match to a person, **2** .... or thing. <u>Underline</u> the key words in the statements and think about possible **3** .... Because the **4** .... will not follow the order of the **5** .... , you will need to **6** .... around the text, looking for paraphrasing of **7** .... words, rather than read the text from **8** .... to end.

Think about it ▸ Reading Worksheet 2: TRUE, FALSE, NOT GIVEN questions

Read the statements. Are they TRUE or FALSE?

1 NOT GIVEN statements are often about information that you may expect to be in the text but is not. ....

2 NOT GIVEN statements never contain words that appear in the text. ....

3 You should make sure that you know what is being referred to in the text before you decide if an idea is given or not. ....

4 The questions are not in the order of the text. ....

5 Use the words given in the statements to help you find the part of the text you need to read carefully. ....

6 If there is no information in the text about the statement, the answer is FALSE. ....

7 TRUE statements agree with the information in the text. ....

8 This question type tests your understanding of the details in the text. ....

 **Think about it** Reading Worksheet 3: Sentence completion

Match the sentence starters (1–8) with the endings (a–h) to make sentences about sentence completion.

1 Read the sentences carefully and <u>underline</u>	**a** have the same meaning as the words in the text.
2 Pay attention to the type	**b** the words before and after the gap.
3 The completed sentences	**c** if the spelling is incorrect.
4 The meaning of the sentence must	**d** than the word limit given in the question.
5 Don't write more words	**e** in the text in any way.
6 Don't change the word	**f** and singular nouns.
7 You will lose marks	**g** must be grammatically correct.
8 Be careful of plural	**h** of word you need to look for in the text.

 **Think about it** Reading Worksheet 4: Short-answer questions

Read the sentences and choose the correct options.

1 The answers *will / will not* follow the order of the text.

2 Answer the questions with *sentences / words* taken from the text.

3 Correct spelling *is / is not* important.

4 You *should / should not* write in full sentences.

5 Make sure you use the *incorrect / correct* information from the text when you answer a question.

6 You *will / will not* lose marks if you change the word in the text.

7 Use the *question word / all the words* in the question to help you decide what type of word you need.

8 If your answer is more words than the word limit, it will be marked *correct / incorrect*.

 **Think about it** Writing Worksheet 1: Letter of complaint

Read the statements about writing a letter of complaint. Are they TRUE or FALSE?

1 The tone of a letter of complaint should be informal and personal.

2 It should include more complex words like 'received' instead of 'got'.

3 It should contain contractions like 'I've' and 'can't'.

4 Using the passive form can make a letter of complaint sound less informal.

5 You should NOT include your address in your answer.

6 Writing over the word limit of 150 words will give you more marks.

7 Aim to write about two of the three bullet points given in the task.

8 Use the task as a checklist to make sure you have answered the question fully.

 **Think about it** Writing Worksheet 2: Job application

Read the sentences and choose the correct options.

1 Use of *formal / informal* style to start and end your letter is essential.

2 Write about *two / all* the three bullet points given in the task.

3 Always *proofread / mark* your answer for grammar, spelling and punctuation errors.

4 The correct ending for a letter which starts 'Dear Sir/Madam' is *Yours faithfully / Yours sincerely*.

5 *Include / Don't include* phases like 'Write soon!' and 'Cheers!'

6 Aim to write a minimum of *150 / 250* words.

7 'I'd be grateful if you could …' is a more formal way or writing *'Please will you … / I want to …'*.

8 The phrase 'I look forward to hearing from you' *can / cannot* be used in a formal letter.

 **Writing Worksheet 3: Personal letter**

Complete the sentences with the words from the box. Use each word once only.

description	exclamations	formal	friendly	full	functions	informal	manager

Personal letters to friends are usually written in an **1** .... style and the tone is
2 .... It is OK to include **3** .... and contractions like 'you'd'
instead of **4** .... forms like 'you had'; however, if you are asked to write a personal
letter to a **5** .... of a shop, for example, the style should be more
6 .... For both types of letter, you will need to show that you can use a range
of language **7** .... , for example, apologising, giving a **8** ....
or asking for information.

 **Writing Worksheet 4: Discussion essay**

Read the sentences. Are they TRUE or FALSE?

1 You do not need to do Writing Part 2 if you have already completed Writing Part 1.

2 You should read the task carefully and make sure you include all the points mentioned.

3 Write your essay in an informal and friendly style.

4 Aim to write no more than 150 words.

5 Your answer should include reasons for your views.

6 Your ideas and views should be supported with examples.

7 Your essay does not need to include a conclusion.

8 Use a range of formal language and grammatical structures.

 **Writing Worksheet 5: Double question essay**

Read the sentences and choose the correct options.

1 There are *one / two* parts to this type of question.

2 You *must / don't have* to answer both parts.

3 You can gain higher marks in coherence and cohesion by using a wider range of *linking words / opinions*.

4 *despite / nevertheless* can be used to contrast two ideas in the same sentence.

5 You *will / will not* be penalised if your answer goes off topic.

6 It is *important / not important* to use a range of vocabulary and grammatical structures accurately.

7 You *don't have / do have* to have an opinion on the question.

8 Organise your writing into clear *notes / paragraphs*.

 **Speaking Worksheet 1: Speaking Part 1**

Complete the text about IELTS Speaking Part 1 with the words from the box. Use each word once only.

correct	dislikes	familiar	five	naturally	penalised	reasons	repeat

In Speaking Part 1, the examiner will ask you questions about **1** .... topics such as your family, friends, hometown or your likes and **2** .... You should try and answer the questions fully and **3** .... , which means that you should give examples and **4** .... to support YES/NO answers. If you ask the examiner to **5** .... the question, you won't be **6** .... ; however, make sure you know the **7** .... way to ask the examiner to say something again and don't do it too often. This part of the test lasts about **8** .... minutes.

 **Think about it** Speaking Worksheet 2: Speaking Part 2

Match the sentence starters (1–8) with the correct endings (a–h).

1 In Part 2, you will be asked to	**a** prepare what you want to say.
2 You will have one minute to	**b** can follow what you are saying.
3 You should aim to talk for	**c** the examiner will ask you one or two follow-up questions.
4 You might be asked to describe an	**d** you to be more coherent.
5 When you have finished your talk,	**e** between one and two minutes.
6 Two criteria you are assessed on are	**f** coherence and fluency.
7 Organise your ideas so the listener	**g** talk about a specific topic.
8 Using the task structure may help	**h** experience, place or person.

 **Think about it** Speaking Worksheet 3: Speaking Part 3

Read the statements about Speaking Part 3. Are they TRUE or FALSE?

1 If the question includes an opinion, you should always agree with it. ....

2 If you are asked about people generally, you should not talk about yourself. ....

3 The Part 3 interview lasts around two to three minutes. ....

4 Giving short YES/NO answers is acceptable. ....

5 You could develop your ideas by offering solutions to problems. ....

6 In Part 3, you should avoid giving factual information. ....

7 One technique for developing ideas is to discuss the advantages or disadvantages of something. ....

8 You can use the phrase 'some might suggest' to present an opinion. ....

EXTENDED ANSWER KEY

Listening Worksheet 1

The underlining indicates where in the track the answers come from.

1

See underlining in Track 1.   1A   2A   3B

> **NARRATOR:** 🔊 **Track 1**
> **Listening Worksheet 1**
>
> **TRUST MANAGER:** Welcome to the Dolphin Conservation Trust and thank you for agreeing to support our charity by working here as volunteers. Before I go through this week's activities, there are a few facts about dolphins I'd like to share with you. First their teeth. As you know, we use ours to bite and chew what we eat, don't we? You might think that's the same for dolphins, but in fact they <u>use theirs for catching what they eat</u>. Then there's sleeping. Did you know that dolphins sleep with half their brain awake and in low levels of alertness? <u>If they didn't do this, they would stop breathing</u>. They can continue swimming while sleeping as well, though digestion has to wait until later. Finally, although their rubbery skin repairs itself quickly, did you know that it damages easily? In fact, it can <u>tear or break from the softest touch</u> on any solid surface.

2

1 'Humans' The speaker says 'we' use ours to bite and chew which refers to humans and not dolphins.

2 'Digestion' The speaker says dolphins can 'continue swimming while sleeping … though digestion has to wait until later', which means digestion does not happen until the dolphin is awake.

3 'Hard' The speaker mentions 'softest' which might have led you to circle 'soft'; however, the speaker says that their skin 'tears or breaks from the softest touch on any solid surface', not that the surfaces are soft.

3

See underlining in Track 2.   C

> **NARRATOR:** 🔊 **Track 2**
> **Listening Worksheet 1**
>
> **TRUST MANAGER:** Right, now I want to tell you about this week's programme. Today is Wednesday and you were going to go to the indoor aquarium, but that project doesn't start until next week, so you

have the rest of the day to relax. Tomorrow, you're off to the sea life hospital where researchers are examining changes in a dolphin's heart rate when they interact with people. Here you will help feed and care for our sick dolphin, Molly. Then, <u>on Friday</u>, you're at the education centre where you'll have the opportunity to <u>assist our part-time biologist with a study</u> that's measuring the amount of carbon dioxide dolphins exhale after they swim. It will be a fantastic experience.

4

1 **project** is a word match for the word 'project' in the question and for incorrect option A.

2 **researchers** is a word match for the word 'research' in the question and for incorrect option B.

4 **help** is a word match for the word 'help' in the question and for incorrect option B.

5

See underlining in Track 3.

> **NARRATOR:** 🔊 **Track 3**
> **Listening Worksheet 1**
>
> **NARRATOR:** 1
> **TRUST MANAGER:** As a sea life charity, it is our <u>purpose to protect</u> all living marine animals.
>
> **NARRATOR:** 2
> **TRUST MANAGER:** We simply must <u>ensure people have a better understanding of impacts</u> that coastal erosion has on sea turtles.
>
> **NARRATOR:** 3
> **TRUST MANAGER:** During their week at the Trust, schoolchildren will <u>participate in various activities</u>.
>
> **NARRATOR:** 4
> **TRUST MANAGER:** You may not know this, but <u>80% of our budget is spent</u> on funding our ocean emergency project.

6a

It used to be <u>controversial</u> among local <u>experts</u>, but thankfully that's been resolved.

6b

Although the speaker says, 'controversial among local experts' which is a paraphrase for A: Experts do not agree, the speaker also says, 'used to' and 'has been resolved'. So although experts did not agree in the past, they do agree now. Also, as A is written using the present tense, it cannot be the correct option.

7

See underlining in Track 4.

1   B is correct as the speaker says, 'It will also be helpful for studies we have planned' which is a paraphrase for 'helping future research'. D is incorrect. The words 'expensive' and 'critical' connect with 'Money' and 'urgently' but the speaker says expensive equipment is not needed.

2   D is correct because the speaker says, 'It's not a quick process' which is a paraphrase for 'takes … a long time'. The word 'technology' in the text is a word match for C but 'out of date' in the text means the opposite of 'new'.

3   C is correct because 'the latest specialist equipment' is a paraphrase for 'uses new technology'. A is incorrect. Although 'controversial among local experts' is a paraphrase for 'Experts do not agree'. The speaker also says, 'used to' and 'has been resolved' so, experts did not agree.

4   F is correct because the speaker says it is popular and specifically among volunteers (unpaid workers).

NARRATOR: **Track 4**
Listening Worksheet 1

TRUST MANAGER: Right, before we finish, I want to briefly mention four of our conservation projects: turtle monitoring; cave mapping; reef surveying and beach clear. OK so, turtle monitoring can be fascinating. It doesn't need expensive equipment and we have already collected some critical data about population numbers. It will also be helpful for studies that we have planned for the future about how the marine life in the area is changing. With cave mapping, we are creating accurate and detailed maps of the local underwater system. It's not a quick process, especially as some of our technology is a little out of date, but it's worthwhile, nevertheless. Next, there's reef surveying. It used to be controversial among local experts, but thankfully that's been resolved. Most surveys are done by divers using the latest specialist equipment to determine the health of the coral ecosystem.
Finally, we have beach cleaning. You'd think it would take ages – we've ten miles of beach to clear of plastic and litter which marine mammals can get caught in – but its popularity among our volunteers means that isn't the case.

---

8   Test task

See underlining in Track 5.

1 and 2

C and E are correct. C is correct because Hannah says, 'The charity uses its money to support campaigns – for example, for changes in fishing policy and so forth.' 'Uses its money to support' is a synonym for 'helps finance'. E is correct because Hannah says, 'volunteers working in observation, office work and other things' which is a synonym for 'help in various ways'.

A is incorrect because children make up '35%' of the membership which is not 'most'.

B is incorrect because the Trust is 'still fairly small compared with the big players'.

D is incorrect because the Trust 'hopes soon to be able to employ its first full-time biologist'. 'hopes soon' refers to a future intention not a present fact.

3

B is correct because Hannah says, 'it has made our activities even more widely publicised and understood'. 'our activities' is a synonym for 'work'.

A is incorrect because although Hannah refers to 'an enormous amount of money' which is a paraphrase for 'extra money', she uses 'not' to show the opposite is the case: the award did **not** bring in extra money.

C is incorrect because Hannah says it may **not** 'bring in extra members' although they hope it will.

4

A is correct because exploration creates 'a lot of noise' which is a synonym for 'sound'.

B is incorrect because Hannah says, 'there'll be little [not very much] pollution'.

C is incorrect because there is 'very little [not very much] water traffic' and although 'companies want to increase exploration', Hannah does not say anything about the movement of ships.

5

B is correct because Hannah talks about a book that she could not put down.

A is incorrect because Hannah says she had 'never seen one'. The word 'home' in the option could mislead as it is a word match for 'dolphins leaving their home' in the text.

C is incorrect because Hannah says nothing about anyone speaking at school. The word 'school' in the option could mislead as it is a word match for 'I hadn't been … interested in them at school' in the text.

6 D is correct because Hannah says that Moondancer has been 'rather elusive since January' and has not 'been sighted'. C is incorrect because although 'most active' has a similar meaning to 'energetic'. Hannah says '**not** the most active' which has the opposite meaning.

7 B is correct because Echo has been 'captured …
on film hundreds of times' which is a synonym for
'photographed frequently'. 'A real character as she
seems to adore', may have led you to 'loving' in A;
however, 'adore' (love) refers to Echo wanting her photo
taken and not to her personality.

8 F is correct because Kiwi's 'particularly large fin on
her back' is a synonym for 'unusual shape'. 'The latest
from the scheme' may have made you consider E;
however, the text refers to giving birth and not to joining
the scheme.

9 C is correct because 'leaping out of the water with
great enthusiasm' is a synonym for 'very energetic'.
Hannah says 'I can picture him doing it now' which
may have led you to B; however, she is referring to
having the image of Samson in her mind, not to taking
photographs.

NARRATOR: **Track 5**
Listening Worksheet 1

INTERVIEWER: Today we're pleased to have on
the show Hannah Wells from the
Dolphin Conservation Trust. Tell us
about the Trust, Hannah.

HANNAH: Well, obviously its purpose is to
protect dolphins in seas all around
the world. It tries to raise people's
awareness of the problems these
marine creatures are suffering
because of pollution and other
threats. It started ten years ago
and it's one of the fastest growing
animal charities in the country –
although it's still fairly small
compared with the big players in
animal protection. We are
particularly proud of the work we do
in education – last year we visited a
huge number of schools in different
parts of the country, going round to
talk to children and young people
aged from five to eighteen. In fact,
about thirty-five per cent of our
members are children.
The charity uses its money to
support campaigns – for example,
for changes in fishing policy and so
forth. It hopes soon to be able to
employ its first full-time biologist –
with dolphin expertise – to monitor
populations. Of course, many
people give their services on a
voluntary basis, and we now have
volunteers working in observation,
office work and other things.

INTERVIEWER: And I believe you've recently won an
award?

HANNAH: Yes, we were really pleased to
win the award from the Charity
Commission last year – for our
work in education. Although it's
not meant an enormous amount
of money for us, it has made
our activities even more widely
publicised and understood. In the
longer term it may not bring in extra
members but we're hoping it'll have
this effect.

INTERVIEWER: Is it possible to see dolphins in UK
waters? I've heard you can see them
in Scotland.

HANNAH: Yes, we have a big project there.
This has long been a haven for
dolphins because it has very
little water traffic. However,
that may be about to change
soon because companies want
to increase exploration there.
We're campaigning against this
because, although there'll be little
pollution, exploration creates a lot
of underwater noise. It means the
dolphins can't rest and socialise.
This is how I became interested
in dolphin conservation in the first
place. I had never seen one and I
hadn't been particularly interested in
them at school. Then I came across
this story about a family of dolphins
who had to leave their home in
the Moray Firth because of the oil
companies and about a child who
campaigned to save them. I couldn't
put the book down – I was hooked.

INTERVIEWER: I'm sure our listeners will want
to find out what they can do to
help. You mentioned the 'Adopt a
Dolphin' scheme. Can you tell us
about that?

HANNAH: Of course! People can choose
one of our dolphins to sponsor.
They receive a picture of it and
news updates. I'd like to tell you
about four which are currently
being adopted by our members:
Moondancer, Echo, Kiwi and
Samson and they are all individual.
First there's Moondancer, not the
most active of the group, he's been

rather elusive since January and hasn't yet been sighted by our observers, but we remain optimistic that he'll be out there soon. Then there's Echo who's our real 'character' as she seems to adore coming up close for the cameras and we've captured her on film hundreds of times. Next, we have Kiwi. The latest from the scheme to give give birth – she's quite shy and came to us after she got caught up in a fishing net. Easily identified by the particularly large fin on her back. Finally, there's Samson – he jumps really high – quite surprisingly so for his age and size really – our youngest member, although almost the longest. Anyway, he's always leaping out of the water with great enthusiasm. I can picture him doing it now. Yes, they're all very different.

INTERVIEWER: Well, they sound a fascinating group …

Listening Worksheet 2

1

1   B

2   C (Distance learning is when you do not attend university, school or college, but study from where you live.)

3   A

2

3   The speaker wants to discuss a work placement.

> **NARRATOR:** 🔊 Track 6
> **Listening Worksheet 2**
>
> **MAN:** Hi Jess, could we catch up on a video call next week? As you know, I'll have finished my second year soon, and I'm thinking about getting some experience in an office. I could really do with your advice …

3

See underlining in Track 7.

1   choose one that's fun

2   make plans for after graduation

3   prove you know the topic in detail

4   don't get lazy

5   ask for some support

> **NARRATOR:** 🔊 Track 7
> **Listening Worksheet 2**
>
> **WOMAN:** Hmm, advice about your work placement … Right … first make sure that you choose one that's fun. There's no point spending a year doing something that you …
> Next, remember it's not about what you are studying now. You need to make plans for after graduation. What I'd suggest is …
> Well, in order to be selected, you must prove you know the topic in detail. There is a lot of competition, and they might choose …
> I'm sure you know this already, but whatever you do, don't get lazy. The company reports back to college, and you don't want …
> Well, It's a really big decision, so before you decide, you might want to ask for some support. I'm sure your tutor will be able to help you …

4

1   in the second year of the course

2   when first choosing where to go

3   when sending your choices

4   when writing your personal statement

5   when doing the year abroad

5

Mia is referring to Question 3. She says, 'send your choices in' which is a signpost for 'sending your choices'.

> **NARRATOR:** 🔊 Track 8
> **Listening Worksheet 2**
>
> **MIA:** Then about six months before you go, you have to send your choices in.

6

See underlining in Track 9.

1   B is the correct answer. Although the speakers say 'places', which might be connected to the word 'travel' in A, Mia tells Josh that students need to get 'good marks' and know the subject well, which are paraphrases for 'show ability in' the subject (Theatre Studies). You know the answer is coming when Mia says, 'second year' (see bold text in Track 9).

JOSH: Hi Mia, I wanted to ask you about the year abroad option. Would you recommend doing that?

MIA: Yes, definitely. It's a fantastic chance to study in another country for a year.

JOSH: I think I'd like to do it, but it looks very competitive – there's only a limited number of places.

MIA: Yes, so next year when you are in the **second year** of the course, you need to work really hard in all your theatre studies modules. Only students with good marks get places – you have to prove that you know your subject really well.

7a

Possible paraphrase ideas:

A   reserve flights and accommodation

C   be punctual / not be late

D   obtain written references

E   organise the last year of study

F   ensure it's the right course for you

G   get assistance

7b

See underlining in Track 10 for the position of the answers and bold text for signposting.

1   B (See Exercise 6)

2   F is correct. Mia talks about 'a programme that would fit in with what I wanted' and then gives course examples to support this idea. This is a paraphrase for 'making sure the course's focus is relevant' in the option.

3   C is correct. Mia talks about 'missing the deadline' and 'getting a move on', which refer to 'being on time' in the option. The word 'friend' in the listening may have drawn you to G 'ask for help'; however, Mia does not mention 'friend' in this context.

4   G is correct. Josh says he will get 'final-year students to give me some tips', which is a way of saying he will 'ask them for help'. The words 'read what they wrote' may have drawn you to D 'letter of recommendation'; however, the context of a recommendation is not mentioned.

5   E is correct. Mia mentions that she 'forgot about the last year' and advises Josh to 'stay in touch so they (the university) know your module choices'. The words 'making arrangements' are misleading word spots for 'make' and 'arrangements' in A.

JOSH: Hi Mia, I wanted to ask you about the year abroad option. Would you recommend doing that?

MIA: Yes, definitely. It's a fantastic chance to study in another country for a year.

JOSH: I think I'd like to do it, but it looks very competitive – there's only a limited number of places.

MIA: Yes, so next year when you are in the **second year** of the course, you need to work really hard in all your theatre studies modules. Only students with good marks get places – you have to prove that you know your subject really well.

JOSH: Right. So how did you **choose where to go**?

MIA: Well, I decided I wanted a programme that would fit in with what I wanted to do after I graduate, so I looked for a programme with emphasis on acting rather than directing for example. It depends on you.

JOSH: OK. Was it easy to get what you wanted?

MIA: Well, about six months before you go, you have to **send in your choices**. I had a friend who missed the deadline and didn't get her first choice, so you do need to get a move on at that stage. You'll find that certain places are very popular with everyone.

JOSH: And don't you have to **write a personal statement** at that stage?

MIA: Yes.

JOSH: Right. I'll get some of the final-year students to give me some tips … maybe see if I can read what they wrote when they applied.

MIA: I think that's a very good idea. I don't mind showing you what I did. And while you're **doing your year abroad**, don't make the mistake I made. I got so involved I forgot all about making arrangements for when I came back here for the last year. Make sure you stay in touch so they know your choices for the optional modules. You don't want to miss out doing your preferred specialisms.

JOSH: Right. That's really helpful …

Get it right!

See underlining in Track 11.

1 actually   2 more useful   3 better off   4 it's best

NARRATOR: **Track 11**
Listening Worksheet 2

NARRATOR: 1
SPEAKER: Well, <u>actually</u> you need to go reception about that.

NARRATOR: 2
SPEAKER: Telephoning the business centre would be <u>more useful</u>.

NARRATOR: 3
SPEAKER: You'd be <u>better off</u> organising it yourself.

NARRATOR: 4
SPEAKER: Hm I understand, but <u>it's best</u> if you wait for them to contact you.

8

See underlining in Track 12.

1 the tutor / tutor
2 'online' / 'checking online' The answer 'business centre' is incorrect. The question asks 'how'.
3 the administrator
4 'wait' The answer 'wait for them' is incorrect because the question says no more than TWO WORDS and 'wait for them' is THREE WORDS.

NARRATOR: **Track 12**
Listening Worksheet 2

NARRATOR: 1
WOMAN: I'm sure the supervisor will help me with my assignment.

MAN: Well, actually you need to go to the office and speak to the <u>tutor</u> about that. Our supervisor may not give you the correct advice.

NARRATOR: 2
WOMAN: I thought I'd go to the library and find out more information.

MAN: Hm … you could, the library has one or two books about the topic, but <u>checking online</u> at the business centre would be a better idea.

NARRATOR: 3
WOMAN: I'm going to ask my mentor about my accommodation later today.

MAN: Well, I went to my mentor for help, but you'd be better off going to the office and talking to the <u>administrator</u>.

NARRATOR: 4
WOMAN: I sent the application last week. I'll chase them when I get home.

MAN: No, it's best if you <u>wait</u> for them to contact you.

---

9   Test task

See underlining in Track 13 for the position of the answers and bold text for signposting.

1 B is correct. Although Alex suggests he can 'find out about a particular company' which connects to F, Eva says, 'You'd be better off', which shows she is going to contradict Alex's idea. Eva then mentions 'using them to talk though what's available', which is a paraphrase for 'discuss options' in the option.

2 F is correct. Eva says, 'make contact with employers and find out more about them', which is a paraphrase for 'obtain company information' in the option.

3 G is correct. Eva says, 'chance of being interviewed' which connects to E; however, she goes on to talk about STEP, suggesting that Alex should go online and 'sign up with them'.

4 A is correct. Alex says, 'keep me informed about the progress of my application', which is a paraphrase for 'get updates' in the option. You may have connected the word 'informed' in the text to the word 'informing' in D; however, this is a misleading word spot. Eva says the mentor works 'with STEP', which connects to G; however, there is no mention of registering.

5 E is correct. Alex tentatively suggests going to the human resources department to 'find out what's going on', which connects with A; however, Eva rejects this by saying 'Not really'. She goes on to say that they will notify Alex if they want him to go for an interview and he will need to 'reply directly and confirm that you can attend'.

6 C is correct. Eva says that Alex will need to contact the tutor if he's been 'offered a job' which connects with D; however, this is because the tutor needs to 'provide a reference'. Eva mentions 'STEP' and 'company' but these are word spots for G and F.

NARRATOR: **Track 13**
Listening Worksheet 2

ALEX: Hi Eva, could you spare a few minutes to talk about the work placement you did last summer?

EVA: Sure. It was a fantastic experience.

ALEX: Yeah, I want to apply for a placement. How do I go about doing it?

EVA:	Well, first I'd go and visit the **careers officer**.
ALEX:	Right, I guess they can help me find out about a particular company?
EVA:	You'd be better off <u>using them to talk though what's available</u>. They've got all the relevant knowledge about the jobs market.
ALEX:	Right, OK.
EVA:	And you could also attend a **work experience fair**. There's one coming up at the end of the month.
ALEX:	Yes, I read about that.
EVA:	Great. Well, they're free for students and you can <u>make contact with employers and find out more about them.</u>
ALEX:	OK. I'll try and go.
EVA:	And then when you know what you want, you need to **go online**.
ALEX:	What's that for?
EVA:	Well, so that you have the best chance of being interviewed, there's an organisation, <u>STEP. You should sign up with them</u>. It's a fairly straightforward process.
ALEX:	Once I've done that, I understand that I'll be assigned a **mentor**. Is that right?
EVA:	Yes, that's right; they work with STEP.
ALEX:	And they will <u>keep me informed about the progress of my application</u>?
EVA:	Spot on.
ALEX:	I don't suppose it's a good idea to get in touch with the **human resource department** directly, is it? You now, to find out what's going on?
EVA:	Not really … but it is them who <u>will notify you if they want you to go for an interview. You'll get an email and, of course, you need to reply directly and confirm you can attend</u>.
ALEX:	Right … So, once I've had an interview, I should let **my tutor** know what the outcome is?
EVA:	Yes, you need to let her know if you've been offered a job so she can <u>provide you with a reference</u>. She knows your academic ability; your qualities, etcetera better than STEP will, and the company are definitely going to ask for one.
ALEX:	Well, thanks very much for the information – I'm starting to look forward …

Listening Worksheet 3

1

1 B is correct. Zack says, 'mainstream films have great special effects'; however, Ellie corrects him by saying, 'they might, but not necessarily'.

2 A is correct. Zack talks about independent films needing prize money and says that he will 'go with that' (choose that answer). Ellie confirms this by saying, 'Correct!'

3 B is correct. Zack mentions 'private investors'; however, this is in the context of independent films and is a word spot for A.

4 A is correct. Ellie mentions 'nine', but goes on to self-correct by saying, 'I … realised just in time that I was about to make a mistake. There are two fewer than I thought', which means there are seven.

NARRATOR: 🔊	**Track 14** **Listening Worksheet 3**
ZACK:	Hey, what are you doing Ellie?
ELLIE:	Oh hi Zack, I've just done this short quiz about films and filmmaking online. I got ten out of ten.
ZACK:	Cool. Let's have a go.
ELLIE:	Sure, right. Let's see, question one, what is a mainstream film? Is it a film with lots of special effects or one produced by a large production company?
ZACK:	Hm, I know this one. Right. Mainstream films have great special effects – I mean like 3D, animation and stuff.
ELLIE:	Well, they might, but not necessarily.
ZACK:	Oh right, so B's the correct answer then.
ELLIE:	That's right.
ZACK:	OK, number two.
ELLIE:	So, this is about film festival competitions. Like, best script or best screenplay. Who enters these, independent or studio films?
ZACK:	Well, I know that independent films need prize money to fund their film productions, so I'm going to go with that.
ELLIE:	Correct! Number three. How are studio films funded?
ZACK:	Well, on the basis that independent films either fund themselves or try and get money from other sources, like private investors, I'd say the studio does it. You know like, Warner Bros or Universal Pictures.

ELLIE:	Correct again! Well done. Next question. How many stages are there in the filmmaking process?
ZACK:	Goodness, how do you expect me to know that?
ELLIE:	It's hard. I thought nine initially but realised just in time that I was about to make a mistake. There are two fewer than I thought.
ZACK:	Hm well, you should know it, you are doing that film studies course. Right next …

2

1 video animation
2 seven / 7 (stages)
3 No. Stage 6 does not have a gap.
4 A singular noun is needed. You know this as the article 'a' comes before the gap.

3

See underlining in Track 15.
1 client

NARRATOR:	🔊 **Track 15** **Listening Worksheet 3**
RIA:	Hi Stan, have you got a minute to talk our work placement? Specifically, the film and video animation project we are working on?
STAN:	Ah animation: the method of creating movement by showing a series of pictures one after the other very quickly.
RIA:	Argggh stop! You sound like our tutor.
STAN:	Ha. Sorry. OK. I'm not too sure about all the stages actually. Let me get a pen so I can write them down. Right: The video animation process.
RIA:	Ready? Good. Well, <u>the first thing is</u> to have a meeting to find out exactly what is required.
STAN:	Right. So we have to get together with the <u>client</u> and get a detailed understanding of the project.

4

See underlining in Track 15.
C 'The first thing is …' tells the listener the speaker is about to talk about their first point.

5

See underlining in Track 16.
2 structure   3 voice   4 drawings   5 colour   6 music

NARRATOR:	🔊 **Track 16** **Listening Worksheet 3**
RIA:	Hi Stan, have you got a minute to talk about our work placement? Specifically, the film and video animation project we are working on?
STAN:	Ah animation: the method of creating movement by showing a series of pictures one after the other very quickly.
RIA:	Argggh stop! You sound like our tutor.
STAN:	Ha. Sorry. OK. I'm not too sure about all the stages actually. First, let me get a pen so I can write them down. Right: The video animation process.
RIA:	Ready? Good. Well, the first thing is to have a meeting to find out exactly what is required.
STAN:	Right. So, we have to get together with the <u>client</u> and get a detailed understanding of the project.
RIA:	Yes. That's right. Next, we **move** on to the idea or concept stage.
STAN:	Right. What happens then?
RIA:	Well, we have to put together a <u>structure</u> for the video that we are going to produce. Then, **once** that's been agreed, we start writing the script.
STAN:	That's really important.
RIA:	Absolutely.
STAN:	So, I've got that. We **then** have to find an actor using one of those online platforms.
RIA:	Right. One with the right sort of <u>voice</u> for our part.
STAN:	Yes. Their appearance doesn't matter as they won't be seen in the video. After **that**, a storyboard is put together. Can you remind me what that is?
RIA:	Well, just think of it as basic <u>drawings</u> which show the progress of the story scene by scene. We include a description of the visuals and the actions too.
STAN:	Great, that's clearer.
RIA:	Then we create the visual style, which means we add <u>colour</u> and things behind the character, like clouds, furniture or pets. This stage can take a long time.
STAN:	When can we get on to the exciting part and get the images moving?
RIA:	The **following** step, animation, is probably my favourite. Everything starts to come to life.

STAN: Is that the end?

STAN: Almost. Before we **finish**, we can set the mood by adding the right <u>music</u>. This is important, so even though it's the last stage, it needs to be done carefully.

STAN: Right, how about we …

6

See bold text in Track 16.

1 move   2 once   3 then   4 that
5 following   6 finish

7

See underlining in Track 17.

1 illustrate   2 final   3 words   4 looked
5 begin   6 talked

NARRATOR: 🔊 **Track 17**
Listening Worksheet 3

RIA: To <u>illustrate</u> this point, let me tell you about what I did at the film studio.

STAN: This brings me to my <u>final</u> point, which is the development of special effects.

RIA: So, in other <u>words</u>, the reason I chose film studies was because …

STAN: OK, so we've <u>looked</u> at the challenges of scriptwriting …

RIA: I'd like to <u>begin</u> by describing the film production process.

STAN: I've <u>talked</u> about the role of the director …

8

A 2 and 5   B 1   C 3   D 4 and 6

9   Test task

See underlining in Track 18.

1   'script' is correct. The speaker says, 'an idea is turned into', which is a paraphrase for 'development of' in the question. Although the speaker mentions nouns, such as 'films', these are all plural nouns and the article 'a' before the gap tells you the answer must be a singular noun.

2   'planning' is correct. The speaker says, 'narrowed down' which is a paraphrase for 'reduced' in the question.

3   'managers' is correct. The words 'are employed' in the question indicate you are listening for a job title in the plural form. The speaker mentions 'producer'; however, this is a singular form. Also, the speaker goes on to say the producer is 'already in place' which means already employed.

4   'budget' is correct. The speakers say, 'It's really important that the company sticks to agreed

activities' which is a paraphrase for a 'schedule must be followed' in the question.

5   'Communication' is correct. As with Question 4, this question is in the **production** stage of the process. The speaker uses the phrase, 'In addition' to tell you that the answer is coming. The word 'crucial' in the text is a paraphrase for 'very important' in the question.

6   'wages' is correct. The speaker says, 'Now let's turn to' to signal that they are changing topic and moving to the next stage: photography. The words, 'things get particularly costly at this point' are a paraphrase for 'An expensive stage' in the question.

7   'remote' is correct. The speaker says, 'filming might be in locations' which is a paraphrase for 'filming in … places'.

8   'suppliers' is correct. The speaker says, 'Once that's done' to signpost that they are moving to the next stage. The speaker mentions 'the company'; however, 'the company' is incorrect because it is two words and 'to company' is not grammatically correct.

9   'studio' is correct. Before the gap, the words 'in the' suggest that you are listening for a place.

10   'cinemas' is correct. Although there is not direct paraphrase for 'are sent to' in the question, 'over the internet', is a paraphrase for 'online platforms'. The word 'films' fits grammatically; however, it cannot be the correct answer because 'Films are sent to films' does not make sense.

NARRATOR: 🔊 **Track 18**
Listening Worksheet 3

LECTURER: Hello everyone and welcome to this afternoon's short presentation about film production. Before we start, I just want to remind you that after the presentation, the university film club will be showing photographic images from their project, 'Films Through The Ages', so please do stay for that if you can. OK right, so coming back to this afternoon's topic, film production, you can see from the slide that there are seven stages.

Now, although production projects are not all the same, they typically start with development. Not all ideas for films start out as original concepts – they may, for instance, come from books, other films or true stories. But in each case, an idea is turned into a <u>script</u> and after approval, writers come up with an initial outline of the film.

Moving on, we come to pre-production. At the start of this stage, the company has a number of different production options. Once these have been narrowed down, planning begins; the vision of the project is decided, and then the producer, who is already in place, is in a position to hire managers and decide where they are going to film.

This brings us to production. During this stage, decisions are made about how the company intends to film day to day

It's really important that the company sticks to agreed activities so that it doesn't exceed its budget – everything has to be well-controlled. In addition, if the process is to run smoothly, it's crucial that there's communication with everyone involved in the process.

Now let's turn to photography – when the camera finally starts to roll. As you can imagine, things get particularly costly at this point. There are wages to consider, filming might be in locations which are remote and difficult to get to, and there are special effects which are becoming more and more technical.

Once that's done, we've got the period immediately after filming, which is called the 'wrap'. This is when the set gets taken down and put away, the site is cleared and suppliers get back anything the company borrowed or hired.

After this we have postproduction. The film is taken back, typically to the studio, to where it is viewed and edited before the final stage of the process, which is what I want to talk briefly about now.

This is distribution. Of course, the film must be distributed for the producers to make a profit, or at least to get back their original investment. Of course, by the time we come to view films in cinemas or quite possibly these days, over the internet, we might forget all the hard work that went into making them. Right, that's the seven stages in the process I wanted to highlight today; you'll find more details in the reading I gave you …

Listening Worksheet 4

1

1   B A fork in the road (or river) is when it divides into two parts.

2   C You might hear 'round the bend' or 'round the corner'.

3   A You might hear 'junction', 'crossroads' or 'intersection'.

2a

1 Map C

NARRATOR: 🔊 Track 19
           Listening Worksheet 4

MAN: Excuse me. Where is Maybrook School?

WOMAN: OK, so this is Main Street …

MAN: Yes, I've just come from the bus station round the corner on Hallam Road.

WOMAN: OK, well, go along Main Street, past the museum, until you come to a hotel on the corner. Take a right at the lights – that's Mill Street. You can't miss the school – it's just past the park opposite the carpark.

2b

1   go along
2   Take a right
3   just past

Get it right!

1 up   2 through   3 round   4 over   5 rear
6 centre   7 before   8 alongside

NARRATOR: 🔊 Track 20
           Listening Worksheet 4

MAN: OK, so you need to walk up this road until you reach the lights.

WOMAN: Once in the main hall you need to go through the door on the right.

MAN: Just round the bend you will find the coffee shop.

WOMAN: Go over the bridge and into the forest.

MAN: You have to enter via the rear of the building.

WOMAN: You'll find the fountain in the centre of the park.

MAN: Just before you reach the lake, there is the picnic area.

WOMAN: The river runs alongside the railway line so you can see it from the train.

3

See underlining in Track 21.

1 D is correct. The correct option is G: opposite the school, just to the right of the beautiful park.

2 C is correct: it is halfway down Main Street directly opposite the surgery.

3 A is incorrect. A is at the end of Mill Street; however, it is next to the bus station. E is the correct answer: just behind the museum at the far end of Mill Street.

NARRATOR: 🔊 **Track 21**
Listening Worksheet 4

MAN: Here's the map of the town centre. It's not to scale, of course, but anyway on the map, you can see the school on Main Street and the bank is <u>opposite the school, just to the right of the beautiful park</u>. There's a great play area there for kids. OK if you need refreshments, there's a coffee shop located <u>halfway down Main Street directly opposite the surgery</u>. It's open seven days a week and the homemade cakes are great. Finally, then, there's the new science centre <u>just behind the museum at the far end of Mill Street</u>. OK that's all I wanted to say for now …

4

See underlining in Track 22.

1 just to the right of   2 on the corner   3 halfway down

NARRATOR: 🔊 **Track 22**
Listening Worksheet 4

MAN: Firstly, we'll plant mature pine trees to provide shelter and shade <u>just to the right of</u> the supermarket …

To address the traffic problems, the pavements <u>on the corner of</u> Carberry Street and Thomas Street will be widened …

Something we're planning to do to help control the flow of traffic in the area is to install traffic lights <u>halfway down</u> Hill Street …

5

See underlining in Track 23.

1 C '<u>just to the right of the supermarket in Days Road</u>'

2 D 'the pavements <u>on the corner of Carberry and Thomas Street</u>'

3 G 'the roadway <u>at the entry of Thomas Street from Days Road</u> will be painted red'

4 B 'A "keep clear" sign will be erected <u>at the junction of Evelyn Street and Hill Street</u>.'

5 F 'install traffic lights <u>halfway down Hill Street where it crosses Days Road</u>'

6 A '<u>on the other side of Hill Street from the supermarket</u>'

7 E '<u>at the other end of Hill Street close to the intersection with Carberry Street</u>'

NARRATOR: 🔊 **Track 23**
Listening Worksheet 4

MAN: Now, we've also put together a map which we've sent out to all the residents in the area. And on the map, we've marked the proposed changes. Firstly, we'll plant mature pine trees to provide shelter and shade <u>just to the right of the supermarket in Days Road</u>.

To address the traffic problems, the pavements <u>on the corner of Carberry and Thomas Street will be widened</u>. This will help to reduce the speed of vehicles entering Thomas Street.

We think it's very important to separate the local residential streets from the main road. So, the roadway <u>at the entry of Thomas Street from Days Road</u> will be painted red. This should mark it more clearly and act as a signal for traffic to slow down.

One way of making sure that the pedestrians are safe is to increase signage at the intersection. <u>A 'keep clear' sign will be erected at the junction of Evelyn Street and Hill Street</u>, to enable traffic to exit at all times.

Something we're planning to do to help control the flow of traffic in the area is to install traffic lights <u>halfway down Hill Street where it crosses Days Road</u>.

Now we haven't thought about only the cars and traffic, of course; there's also something for the children. We're going to get school children in the area to research a local story, the life of a local sports hero perhaps, and an artist will incorporate that story into paintings on the wall of a building <u>on the other side of Hill Street from the supermarket.</u>

And finally, we've agreed to build a new children's playground which will be <u>at the other end of Hill Street close to the intersection</u> with Carberry Street.

6

1 in the southeast   2 in the far northwest
3 to the east   4 south of
5 just on the west   6 near the north

7 Test task

See underlining in Track 24.

1. A 'there's a lake in the northwest of the park, with a bird hide to the west of it, at the end of a path'
2. I 'close to where refreshments are available … in the southern part of the park, leading off from the path'.
3. F 'the circular area on the map surrounded by paths'
4. E 'in the western section of the park, between two paths'
5. D 'along the path which takes you to the east gate'

NARRATOR:	Track 24 Listening Worksheet 4
PARK CO-ORDINATOR:	Hello everyone. I'd like to tell you about our new wildlife area, Hinchingbrooke Park, which will be opened to the public next month. This slide doesn't really indicate how big it is, but anyway, you can see the two gates into the park, and the main paths.
	As you can see, there's a lake in the northwest of the park, with a bird hide to the west of it, at the end of a path. So it'll be a nice quiet place for watching the birds on the water.
	Fairly close to where refreshments are available, there's a dog-walking area in the southern part of the park, leading off from the path.
	And if you just want to sit and relax, you can go to the flower garden; that's the circular area on the map surrounded by paths.
	For those who want some shade, there's a wooded area in the western section of the park, between two paths.
	If you need to use the facilities, the toilet block is located just along the path which takes you to the east gate. It's right on the path so you can't miss it. OK, that's enough from me, so let's go on to …

Listening Worksheet 5

1

See underlining in Track 25.

They've all inspired modern technology.

NARRATOR:	Track 25 Listening Worksheet 5
ANNA:	Hi Kennie, what are you up to?
KENNIE:	Hi Anna, I'm just reading an article online. Here, look at these photos and tell me what the connection is.
ANNA:	Erm, Well, they're not people? They're all found in the wild?
KENNIE:	Nope. You'll never guess.
ANNA:	Go on then … tell me.
KENNIE:	They've all, in different ways, inspired advances in modern technology.
ANNA:	Really? Wow, tell me more …

Get it right!

a and b

1, 2, 3 and 4 are incorrect because the candidate made simple mistakes.

A 1 and 2 For Question 1, 'River walk' might be the correct answer; however, the instructions say NO MORE THAN TWO WORDS and the candidate has written THREE words. For Question 2, the answer might be 'small' as it fits grammatically; however, the candidate included a number (£10) which was not included in the instructions. If you need to listen for numbers, the instructions will include AND/OR A NUMBER.

B 4 The base word 'camera' might be correct; however, it does not fit grammatically – we know this because the plural verb 'are' just before the gap tells us a plural noun is needed. The candidate probably heard the word 'cameras' but wrote 'camera' in error.

C 3 The heading of this column is 'Event', so the answer 'Wednesday', which is a day not an event, is incorrect. The candidate probably didn't use the headings to help them predict the answers and follow the speaker as they were listening.

2

1 ~~book~~ 2 ~~concern~~ 3 ~~boys~~ 4 ~~girl~~ 5 ~~museum~~

6 ~~days~~ 7 ~~dog~~ 8 ~~animal~~ 9 ~~idea~~ 10 ~~things~~

3

3. What could be on a gecko's feet? (plural noun) What part of a gecko's foot might be sticky?
4. What things do climbers use? (plural noun) What things have been made for climbers? Shoes? Ropes?

5 Where do kingfishers go? What do kingfishers do? (verb). What do kingfishers need their beaks for? Eat?

6 Where do the trains go?

4

See underlining in Track 26.

1 'skin'

2 'boats' Kennie mentions 'spaceships' but then uses the word 'actually' to signpost that he is going to correct that idea.

3 'hairs' Kennie uses the phrase 'thousands of' which tells you it must be a plural noun and not a singular one.

4 'gloves' The words 'developed special' without an article, 'a' or 'the', indicate that you are listening for a plural or uncountable noun. In the table, a singular noun will not fit grammatically ('have been made', not 'has been made').

5 'dive' The verb 'catch' is mentioned; however, this is in connection with 'food' and not with doing something 'silently' (so it can catch food).

6 'tunnels' The words 'when the trains went through' without an article, 'a' or 'the', indicate you need a plural or uncountable noun.

NARRATOR: 🔊 **Track 26**
Listening Worksheet 5

ANNA: Hi Kennie, what are you up to?

KENNIE: Hi Anna, I'm just reading an article online. Here, look at photos and tell me what the connection is?

ANNA: Erm, Well, they're totally different. Hm … they're not people? They're all found in the wild?

KENNIE: Nope. You'll never guess.

ANNA: Go on then … tell me.

KENNIE: They've all inspired modern technology.

ANNA: Really? Wow, tell me more.

KENNIE: OK, so let's start with this one.

ANNA: A shark! So why are scientists interested in them? Is it their teeth?

KENNIE: No. It's because they've got a pattern – not exactly scales, but a bit like that, all over their skin. This helps them to move easily and smoothly through the water because nothing can attach to it. Anyway, scientists from NASA became aware of this and decided to copy it. You'd think it'd be for spaceships – you know for coming through the atmosphere – but actually it's for boats to help them move faster.

ANNA: That makes sense, I guess.

KENNIE: Then there's geckos …

ANNA: Well, I know that they have light-sensitive eyes.

KENNIE: Yes, they're able to make various sounds to communicate, too. Anyway, they've got thousands of hairs on the bottom of their feet so they can climb without falling. They can even walk on smooth ceilings or climb up glass walls. And as well as that, scientists have already developed special gloves for rock climbers based on the same principle and they hope one day to be able to catch rubbish in space.

ANNA: That would be cool. What about the kingfisher – such a beautiful bird.

KENNIE: It is. Right, well a kingfisher's habitat is slow-flowing rivers and lakes. Because they have an aerodynamic beak – pointed and shaped like a spear – when they dive into water to catch food, it's noiseless. A bird-loving Japanese engineer redesigned the high-speed bullet trains using the same idea. The problem they were having with loud booms when the trains went through tunnels disappeared.

ANNA: Goodness. How interesting. Let's find out what other animals have inspired …

---

5 Test task

See underlining in Track 27.

1 'Frogs' The speaker says, 'The first species to generate a lot of interesting information was frogs.' The omission of an article ('a' or 'the') indicates a plural form is needed.

2 'owls' The speaker mentions the phrase 'urban areas', which is a paraphrase for 'in cities' in the table.

3 'count' The phrase 'no difficulties with our efforts to precisely' is a paraphrase for 'Easy to … accurately' in the table.

4 'seeds' The phrase 'a variety of' in the table indicates you need a plural noun. The plural noun 'plants' is mentioned by the speaker; however, the plants produce the seeds which the birds eat: 'buying lots of different plants meaning there's an extensive range of seeds around, which is what they feed on'.

5 'survey' The speaker uses the word 'massive', which is a synonym for 'large' in the table and 'about to be launched' means 'starting soon'.

6 'chemicals' The speaker says, 'Populations have recovered', which tells you the answer is coming (if you are using the headings to help you). The speaker's phrase 'decline from …' indicates something has been reduced (less use of).

7 'online' The speaker does not use a synonym for the word 'watch' in the table; however, they say, 'A webcam, originally installed for security purposes, now streams the pair's activities online' which implies that people watch the birds and that they do this online.

NARRATOR: 🔊 Track 27 Listening Worksheet 5

TEACHER: Good morning. Today I'd like to present the findings of our Year 2 project on wildlife found in gardens throughout our city. The first species to generate a lot of interesting information was <u>frogs</u>. And there was a clear pattern here – they breed where there is water that's suitable. Garden ponds are on the rise, and rural ponds are disappearing, leading to massive migration to the towns. Hedgehogs are also finding it easier to live in urban areas – this time because <u>owls</u>, for example, that hunt hedgehogs at night, prefer not to leave the protection of their rural environment. We had lots of sightings, so all in all, we had no difficulties with our efforts to precisely <u>count</u> their numbers.

Our next species is the finest of bird singers, the song thrush. On the decline in the countryside, they are experiencing a revival in urban gardens because these days gardeners, like myself actually, are buying lots of different plants meaning there's an extensive range of <u>seeds</u> around, which is what they feed on.

Another factor is the provision of nesting places – which is actually better in gardens than the countryside. Hard to believe it, but it's true. Incidentally, we discovered that a massive new <u>survey</u> on their numbers is about to be launched, so you should keep an eye open for that.

Next, I'd like to talk about the peregrine falcon – the fastest bird in the world that can reach astonishing speeds of three hundred and twenty kilometres an hour. Populations have recovered following decades of decline from harmful <u>chemicals</u> used in farming and they now nest in over two hundred artificial or urban locations in the country. Nottingham Trent University's Newton building is home to one of the most famous pairs of peregrine falcons.

A webcam, originally installed for security purposes, now streams the pair's activities <u>online</u>. Right well, that's all I wanted to talk about this evening; however, please do stay for our spectacular photographic display when I'll be around to answer any questions you may have.

Listening Worksheet 6

1

See underlining in Track 28.

1 help 2 information 3 details 4 order 5 time
6 blank 7 Change

NARRATOR: 🔊 Track 28 Listening Worksheet 6

JODIE: Hey, how's it going?

FRANK: Alright thanks. I'm just revising for my IELTS test.

JODIE: Me too! I'm worried about note completion questions. Can you give me some advice?

FRANK: Of course. Let me think. OK, first I'd suggest you **read the title and subtitles**. This will <u>help</u> you to follow what the speaker is saying.

JODIE: Got it.

FRANK: Then, it's important that you **consider**, for each question, the <u>information</u> that fits. So, if it could be a number, person, location or something else.

JODIE: OK. Understood. What else?

FRANK: Well, this part of the test is about testing your ability to listen for <u>details</u> not the general idea.

JODIE: That's hard.

FRANK: Yes, it is, but **don't forget that the questions** follow the same order as the listening text, so that makes it a bit easier.

JODIE: Right and what shouldn't I do?

FRANK: Well, you have thirty seconds or so to look at the questions **during the test**. Some people just look out the window, but that's really not a useful way to spend the time you have! Instead, you should study the questions and think about what the speaker might say.

JODIE: That's a good point.

FRANK: It is. Hm … right, next I'd say, **if you don't know** an answer, think about the meaning of the passage as a whole and write down something that might be possible. You might still get a mark. Obviously, you get no marks if a question is left blank.

JODIE: OK – I hadn't thought of that. Anything else?

FRANK: Hmm … yes *one more thing* and this is really important. Candidates sometimes change the verb tense or make a plural a singular and that's a *big mistake*. You must write exactly what you hear.

JODIE: Really, so if the speakers says, for example, 'house' and I write 'houses', or 'frogs' and I write 'frog', then it is wrong?

FRANK: Yep – that would usually be a wrong answer!

JODIE: Cool. That's really useful advice thanks …

2

See bold text in Track 28.

1 read the title and subtitles
2 consider
4 don't forget that the questions
5 during the test
6 if you don't know

3

See italic text in Track 28.

1 B The speaker says 'one more thing' to tell the listener that they are moving to their final point after all the other things they've said.

4 Possible paraphrases:

2 electronically
3 thinking of / inventing / having an idea / a plan for an object / a gadget
4 differently / in a different way
5 the same / not different   boring / dull

5

Sentence 2 – something belonging to Jonas connected to a competition

Sentence 3 – place / room

Sentence 4 – object connected to Jonas' design

Sentence 5 – some existing objects (maybe the things Jonas is focusing on / redesigning)

6a

See underlining in Track 29.

'tutor' We predicted the type of word needed for the first gap was a person. While two people are mentioned by Jonas, 'professor' and 'tutor', the phrase 'give me some support' is what the tutor said to Jonas, *not* what the professor said.

6b

See underlining in Track 29.   2 drawings

3 kitchen   4 technology   5 dishwashers

NARRATOR: 🔊 **Track 29**
Listening Worksheet 6

JONAS: Erm … hello Professor. I'm working on my entry for the Global Design Competition. My tutor said you might be able to give me some support.

PROFESSOR: Ah, yes, I got an electronic copy of your drawings. Come in and tell me about it. What sort of competition is it?

JONAS: Well, it's an international design competition and we have to come up with a new idea for a typical domestic kitchen appliance.

PROFESSOR: I see, and are there any special conditions? Does it have to save energy for example?

JONAS: Actually, that was the focus last year. This year's different. We have to develop an innovative idea for existing technology, using it in a way that hasn't been thought of before.

PROFESSOR: I see, that sounds tricky. And what have you chosen?

JONAS: Well, I decided to choose dishwashers because they are an everyday item in most Australian houses, but they're all pretty boring and almost identical to each other.

I think some people will be prepared to pay a little extra for something that looks different.

PROFESSOR: That's a nice idea …

---

7   Test task

See underlining in Track 30.

1   'starting' You know the answer is coming when you hear the professor and Jonas say the word 'stone'. 'The dishwasher' in the listening text is a paraphrase for 'the machine' in the question.

2   'clean' You know the answer is coming when Jonas says 'carbon dioxide'. The 'plates and cups' is a paraphrase for 'the dishes' in the question.

3   'waste' You know the answer is coming when you hear 'once the washing cycle is complete' in the listening text which is a paraphrase for 'At the end of the washing cycle' in the question.

4   'potential' 'reduce household costs' in the question is a paraphrase for 'save … money on their electricity bills' in the listening text. The listening text mentions the design is also 'good for the planet', but this what Jonas's tutor thinks (not what Jonas thinks).

5   'presentation' Jonas says, 'I was hoping you could help me with', which is a paraphrase for 'needs help' preparing for' in the question.

6   'model' Jonas's professor says, 'if you want to stand a good chance of winning you really need a …', which is a way of giving advice.

7   'materials' Jonas's professor asks, 'What is the main difficulty so far?', which tells you the answer is coming. The professor then suggests 'materials'. We know Jonas agrees because he says, 'Yes. I want it to look professional, but everything that's top quality is also very expensive.'

8   'grant' The professor says, 'why don't you talk to the university about', which is a way of making a suggestion.

9   'details' The professor asks Jonas to give him the report which implies that the professor is going to 'check' it. The word 'technical' is incorrect because it is an adjective and a noun ('the___') is needed in the gap.

NARRATOR: 🔊 **Track 30**
Listening Worksheet 6

PROFESSOR: I see you've called your design 'the Rockpool'; why is that?

JONAS: Basically, because it looks like the rockpools you find on a beach. The top is made of glass so that you can look down into it.

PROFESSOR: And there's a stone at the bottom. Is that just for decoration?

JONAS: Actually, it does have a function. Instead of pushing a button, you turn the stone.

PROFESSOR: So it's really just a novel way of starting the dishwasher.

JONAS: That's right.

PROFESSOR: It's a really nice design, but what makes it innovative?

JONAS: Well, I decided to make a dishwasher that uses carbon dioxide.

PROFESSOR: In place of water and soap? How will you manage that?

JONAS: The idea is to pressurise it so that it becomes a liquid. The fluid is then released into the dishwasher so it can clean the plates and cups, etcetera, all by itself.

PROFESSOR: Sounds like a brilliant idea! Your system will totally stop the need for strong detergents, like soap. So, what happens once the washing cycle is complete?

JONAS: Well, to allow the contents to dry, the waste all goes to an area called the holding chamber. That's where the liquid is depressurised and changes back to a gas. Then the oil and grease are separated out and removed.

PROFESSOR: It sounds like you've thought it all out very thoroughly. So, do you think it'll ever be built?

JONAS: I don't see why not. It's energy efficient and has the potential to save people quite a bit of money on their electricity bills. My tutor pointed out that as it uses no harmful chemicals, it's good for the planet too.

PROFESSOR: Well, I'm sure a lot of positive things will come out of your design.

PROFESSOR: Now, you seem to have thought about everything so what exactly did you need me to help you with?

JONAS: Well, it's my final design submission, I've made it to the final stage of the competition, and, in a few months' time, I have to give a presentation, and that's the part I was hoping you could help me with.

PROFESSOR: Right, well that should be easy enough. What have you managed to do so far?

JONAS: Well, I've got detailed drawings to show how it will work and I've also written a five-hundred-word paper on it.

PROFESSOR: I see. Well, if you want to stand a good chance of winning, <u>you really need a model of the machine</u>.

JONAS: Yes, I thought I might but I'm having a few problems.

PROFESSOR: What is the main difficulty so far? Let me guess – is it the <u>materials</u>?

JONAS: Yes. I want it to look professional, but everything that's <u>top quality is also very expensive</u>.

PROFESSOR: Look, projects like this are very important to us. They really help lift our profile. So why don't you talk to the university about a <u>grant</u>? I can help you <u>fill out the application forms</u> if you like.

JONAS: That would be great.

PROFESSOR: You'd better show me this paper you've written as well. For a global competition such as this, you need to <u>make sure the technical details you've given are accurate and thorough</u>.

JONAS: That would be a great help.

PROFESSOR: Is there anything else I can do?

JONAS: Well, no I think that's it. Thanks, you've been really helpful …

Reading Worksheet 1

1

Method of cleaning 4 All its parts can go in the <u>dishwasher</u>
Speed is the item not needed.
Durability (how long it will last) 8 It is designed to <u>last a long time</u>
Colour 1 It is available in a range of <u>colours</u>.
Level of noise 2 It is <u>noisy</u> when in use.
Appearance 5 It is particularly <u>attractive</u>.
Size 6 It <u>takes up a lot of space</u>. This phrase means that the juicer is quite big.
Extras 7 Some <u>extras</u> are included.

2

1 B (A is incorrect because 'costs a lot' means 'expensive'.)

2 A (B is incorrect because 'wins first prize for its looks' means that it IS attractive.)

3 A (B is incorrect because 'built to stand the test of time' means that it is durable and will NOT need replacing before long.)

4 B (A is incorrect because only two colours are mentioned – black and grey.)

5 B (A is incorrect because 'NOT dishwasher friendly' means that it can't be put in the dishwasher.)

6 A (B is incorrect because 'HARDLY makes a sound' means that it isn't noisy.)

7 B (A is incorrect because 'compact' refers to something that is small in size.)

8 A (B is incorrect as 'in next to no time' refers to doing something fast or quickly.)

3

C: <u>A range of colours</u> means at least three colours – so several colours.
B, C, D, E and F mention colour:
B: 'Choose from <u>cool blue or bright pink</u>.'
C: 'It comes in <u>black or grey</u>.'
D: 'comes in <u>bright yellow, red, blue or green</u>'
E 'It's available in a <u>choice of two colours</u> – we liked the <u>pale blue one</u> best'
F: 'This <u>pastel green juicer</u>'
D mentions four colours – a range. (F is incorrect because it mentions only one colour; B, C and E are also incorrect because they mention only two colours.)

4

2 It is <u>noisy</u> when <u>in use</u>.

B, C and F mention level of noise. B says, 'and it's <u>quiet too – unlike some other models which sound like a small jet taking off</u>'. C says, 'It's a <u>bit loud</u> though, <u>so keep the door shut when you're using it</u>.' And F says, 'And <u>the noise is minimal</u> compared with other juicers too.'
C is correct. (B and F are incorrect because they are quiet and don't make much noise'.)

5

3 It <u>costs less</u> than some other juicers.

A, B and E refer to cost. A says, 'If you're looking for a <u>reasonably priced juicer</u>'. B says, 'This <u>isn't the cheapest juicer around</u>' And E says, '<u>This juicer is pricey</u>'. A is correct because it was described to have a 'reasonable' price, this means the price is considered fair. B and E are incorrect because they are described as not cheap and 'pricey', meaning expensive.

4 <u>All its parts</u> can go <u>in the dishwasher</u>.

A, B, C, D and F make reference to how the parts can be washed.

A: '<u>All its key parts come apart for washing by hand</u>'

B: '<u>Each of its parts is dishwasher friendly</u>'

C: '<u>The parts need to be washed in the sink</u> but they'll come out gleaming'.

D: '<u>The cutting blades need hand washing, but the rest of the parts are dishwasher safe</u>.'

F: 'there's a special cleaning brush for washing each of its parts by hand'

B is correct. (A, C and F are incorrect because none of the parts can be put in dishwasher. D is also incorrect because only SOME of the parts are suitable for a dishwasher.)

5   It is <u>particularly attractive</u>.

A and E refer to appearance.

A: '<u>While it doesn't win first prize for its looks</u>'

E: '<u>it's a thing of beauty with its stylish curved lines</u>'.

E is correct. (A is incorrect because 'it doesn't win first prize for its looks' means it isn't attractive.)

6   It takes up <u>a lot of space</u>.

A, B, C, D and E refer to size and space needed.

A: 'it does have <u>a space-saving design, which means it's tall rather than bulky</u>'

B: '<u>It's on the large size though</u>, so unless you have a kitchen to match, consider another model.'

C: '<u>If you lack space in your kitchen</u> and you're after a juicer to do the basics'

D: '<u>It will fit neatly on your worktop</u>'

E: 'and <u>it's compact enough to keep on the worktop</u>.'

B is correct. (A, C, D and E are all incorrect because they describe juicers that are small in size and take up little space.)

7   Some <u>extras</u> are included.

Only F makes reference to 'extras' or additional items that come with the juicer.

'<u>You even get a few accessories thrown in</u> – there's <u>a special cleaning brush</u> for washing each of its parts by hand, and there's a <u>smoothie and ice cream strainer</u> too.'

F is correct: the extras refer to things that are included free with the juicer – the brush and the strainer – the accessories.

8   It is designed to <u>last a long time</u>.

C and F make reference to 'time'.

C: 'built to stand the test of time and it has survived four years of daily use'

F: 'juicing up your oranges … and other citrus fruits <u>in next to no time</u>'

C is correct. (F is incorrect because 'in next to no time' is not referring to how durable it is, but how quickly the juicer works.)

6   Test task

1 F

'Special is an inclusive <u>return travel package for two people</u> including Sleeper reservations for one or both directions. <u>It can mean savings for both of you</u>.'

The text makes reference to a special travel package

for two people and the advantage is that the cost brings savings.

None of the other texts mention travelling with other people.

2 C

'Available right up to the day of travel and valid any day <u>except these peak days: all Fridays</u>, also 18–30 December, 31 March and 28 May.'

The text says that the ticket cannot be used for travel on Fridays.

G is a distractor, making reference to 'Fridays' saying, 'You are advised to turn up early for travel on a Friday.' But it is possible to use the ticket for travel on that day.

3 G

'Not the cheapest option but <u>available up to the time of travel and valid for all trains and at all times</u>.'

The text says that there are no restrictions and that you can travel on this train whenever you want.

C is a distractor because it mentions that it is 'valid any day' and then goes on to list restrictions – 'except these peak days: all Fridays, also 18–30 December, 31 March and 28 May'.

D is also a distractor because it says, 'This flexible ticket is valid every day', but then states that it can only be used 'on any train between 10am and midnight'. This means that there are restrictions.

4 B

The text says the ticket is 'available by booking at <u>least a week before outward travel</u>'.

This means that it can only be booked up to 7 days before departure.

Text A is a distractor as it says 'book at least 2 weeks ahead'.

5 A

'<u>Only available for travel after 9am</u>. Book at least 2 weeks ahead and travel between Edinburgh or Glasgow and London for <u>the unbeatable price of £59 return</u>.'

The text makes reference to the 'unbeatable price of £59 return' which means it is the cheapest ticket available. It also mentions a restriction on departure time '<u>Only available for travel after 9am</u>'.

Text F is a distractor as it mentions 'savings for both of you'. Text G is also a distractor because it says it is 'not the cheapest option', but this means that the ticket is expensive rather than cheap.

6 A

The text says, 'This ticket is non-refundable unless the service is cancelled.' This means that you can't get your money back if you decide not to travel. This would only happen if the train you were due to travel on was cancelled.

B is a distractor because it makes reference to refunds being available. It says, 'Ticket refundable on payment of a 25% administrative charge'. This means you would get some of your money back if you decided not to travel.

7 E

It is not possible to use this ticket if you want to travel on a Monday and return the following day (on a Tuesday). The text says, 'The journey must include a Saturday night away'.

No other texts make specific reference to 'Monday' so there are no distractors for this question.

8 D

The text says that the ticket is valid for travel between 10am and midnight. It is not valid between midnight and 10am. 'Your ticket allows standard class travel on any train between 10am and midnight.'

C is a distractor as it makes reference to travel being available between midnight and 2am. 'Departures between midnight and 2am count as previous day's departures.'

Reading Worksheet 2

1

1 4: Paragraph 4 gives details about the lighthouse. We learn two facts about it: it has '77 steps' and that 'it was once the brightest lighthouse in the southern hemisphere'.

2 5: Paragraph 5 advises people what items of clothing and footwear to bring on the trip. 'Please bring suitable walking shoes, a light raincoat, sunscreen and a hat.'

3 1: Paragraph 1 gives examples of birds that can be seen on the island 'It is home to many native birds, including the colourful takahe, and the New Zealand robin and fernbird.'

4 4: Paragraph 4 gives information about the refreshments available in the visitor centre. The text says, 'Complimentary tea and coffee is provided at the centre'.

5 4: Paragraph 4 gives information about the walking trails – we learn that there are several of these on the island. The text says, 'you can explore the walking trails that wind throughout the island'.

6 2: Paragraph 2 gives information about what is covered in the orientation. The text says, 'You will receive a short orientation, where you will learn about the deforestation of the island and environmental recovery efforts since 1984'.

2

1 1.5 hours (Paragraph 3: 'You can then opt to take a 1.5-hour guided walk')

2 75 minutes (Paragraph 2: 'You will enjoy a 75-minute ferry ride')

3 3 (Paragraph 2: 'and 3 reptile species')

4 77 (Paragraph 4: 'With its 77 steps')

5 1984 (Paragraph 2: 'you will learn about the … environmental recovery efforts since 1984')

3a

1 Restrictions apply to the number of visitors permitted on the island.

2 The orientation is provided by the ranger.

3 The tuatara lizard is now only found on this island.

3b

Overview

Tiritiri Matangi island is a protected sanctuary for rare and endangered animal and bird species of New Zealand. It is home to many native birds, including the colourful takahe, and the New Zealand robin and fernbird. You will have the day to explore the area, where visitor numbers are limited (Question 1) in order to protect the island's wildlife.

What to expect

You will enjoy a 75-minute ferry ride from Auckland across the Hauraki Gulf to the harbour of the reserve. On arrival you will be met with the island's ranger and volunteer guides. You will receive a short orientation, (Question 2) where you will learn about the deforestation of the island and environmental recovery efforts since 1984, which have helped re-establish 12 endangered native bird species and 3 reptile species, including the rare tuatara – a prehistoric lizard. (Question 3)

3c

1 TRUE/T

2 NOT GIVEN/NG

3 NOT GIVEN/NG

3d

Statement 2: There is reference to the ranger in the statement and in the text. We know that the ranger meets the participants on arrival. But the subsequent sentence in the text gives no indication of who provides the orientation. A candidate might assume that it is the ranger that gives the talk.

Statement 3: There is reference to the date of 1984 and the re-establishment of the tuatara on the island. But all we know is that at some point the tuatara was successfully re-introduced on this island. We do not know if it was re-introduced elsewhere. A candidate might assume that this was the only place where it was re-introduced.

4a

4 Trip participants are expected to join the walking tour.

5   Trip participants <u>are allowed to touch the displays in the visitor centre</u>.

6   <u>Food</u> is available for participants to <u>purchase on the island</u>.

7   Participants <u>have the opportunity to climb to the top of the lighthouse</u>.

8   Some trails are <u>suitable for inexperienced walkers</u>.

<u>You can then opt to take a 1.5-hour guided walk</u>, which is recommended for an in-depth introduction to the island's wildlife and history, or you can choose to spend the whole day exploring the island on your own.

The guided walk will finish at the visitor centre, <u>where you can browse through informative, interactive exhibits</u>. Complimentary tea and coffee is provided at the centre and there are plenty of tables <u>where you can eat your lunch (not sold on the island so please bring your own)</u>. Afterwards, you can relax on the grounds outside the visitor centre and perhaps check out the island's lighthouse. <u>With its 77 steps, it was once the brightest lighthouse in the southern hemisphere</u>. Alternatively, you can explore the walking trails that wind throughout the island, with <u>varying choices for different fitness levels and experience</u>.

4b

4   FALSE/F – the text says that the guided walk is optional. 'You can then opt to take a 1.5 hour guided walk'

5   TRUE/T – the text says that visitors have access to 'interactive exhibits' – which means that they can touch them.

6   FALSE/F – the text says that food is 'not sold on the island' and that visitors must 'bring your own'.

7   NOT GIVEN/NG – the text mentions that visitors can visit the lighthouse and that it has 77 steps, but it does not say that they can climb the steps to the top.

8   TRUE/T – the text says there are walking trails for 'different fitness levels and experience'. This means that some of the walking trails are appropriate for people who don't do much walking normally.

5   Test task

1   TRUE/T

'<u>Smoke alarms</u> are now a standard feature in Australian homes and <u>are required by the National Building Code in any recently built properties</u>.'

'recently built properties' in the text is a paraphrase for 'all new houses' in the statement. And 'are required' in the text is another way of saying 'must have'.

2   FALSE/F

'There are two principal types of smoke alarms. <u>Ionization alarms are the cheapest</u> and most readily available smoke alarms.'

The text says that ionization smoke alarms 'are the cheapest' so this means they cost less than photoelectric smoke alarms.

3   NOT GIVEN/NG

'Most battery-powered smoke alarms can be installed by the homeowners and do not require professional installation.'

The text says that most smoke alarms can be fitted or 'installed' by homeowners but there is no mention of how long the process of fitting or installation takes.

4   TRUE/T

'For the installation of <u>hard-wired smoke alarms, powered from the mains electricity supply, however, you will need the services of a licensed professional</u>.'

The text says that a 'licensed professional' has to fit a hard-wired smoke alarm. This paraphrases the 'specialist technician' used in the statement.

5   FALSE/F

'If <u>you have fewer than ten ionization alarms to get rid of, you may put them in your domestic waste</u>.'

The text states it is possible to put a quantity of ionization alarms in domestic waste – up to ten of them can be disposed of in the household rubbish.

6   TRUE/T

'<u>Your battery-powered smoke alarm will produce a short beep every 60 seconds to alert you when the battery is running out</u> and needs replacing.'

The text says that the smoke alarm will make a 'beep' sound to indicate that the battery is 'running out', which means the battery power is low.

7   FALSE/F

'Nevertheless, it should be tested <u>every month</u> to ensure that the battery and the alarm sounder are working.'

The text does not say that they need to be checked every two weeks.

Reading Worksheet 3

1

1   spaces

2   work

3   hours

4   machines

5   clothes

6   qualification

2

1   TRUE/T – 'Greenkeepers plant and maintain the grass and turf used for public parks, gardens and sporting areas.'

2   FALSE/F – 'They may also spend some of their time indoors in an office doing some administrative tasks.'

3 TRUE/T – 'They may work long hours every day. This may involve starting their very early in the morning and continuing late into the evening.'

4 TRUE/T – 'Greenkeepers use lawnmowers and other machinery, such as leaf-blowers. They occasionally also operate mini tractors in their work.'

5 FALSE/F – 'They wear protective footwear and overalls as well as gloves and goggles if using toxic chemicals and fertilisers to minimise any associated risks.'

6 FALSE/F – 'It is possible to work as a greenkeeper without formal qualifications.'

3

1 h
2 g
3 d
4 f
5 a
6 c
7 b
8 e

4a

1 Greenkeepers are responsible for <u>mending timber</u> _____.

2 It is important for greenkeepers to ensure that all _____ <u>is removed</u> from the grounds.

3 Greenkeepers ensure that <u>grounds such as soccer</u> _____ <u>are ready</u> for use.

4 Greenkeepers mainly <u>carry out their duties</u> _____.

5 _____ <u>as well as manual work</u> are carried out by greenkeepers.

6 The work of a greenkeeper sometimes involves <u>driving a small</u> _____.

7 When handling <u>dangerous</u> _____, <u>special hand protection</u> must be worn by greenkeepers.

8 The normal <u>duration of a traineeship</u> is _____.

9 Someone who <u>has a relevant</u> _____ <u>may have a better chance of getting a job</u> as a greenkeeper.

4b

- a word and a number?   8
- a singular noun?   2; 6; 9
- an adjective?   5
- an adverb?   4
- a plural noun?   1; 3; 7

5

Adam: 'fence' is incorrect because the plural form of the noun is needed for the sentence to be correct grammatically.

Beatrice: 'gates' is incorrect because these are referred to in the text as made of metal. They are not made of 'timber', which is a synonym for 'wooden'.

6

1 fences
2 debris
3 pitches
4 outdoors
5 Administrative
6 tractor
7 chemicals
8 12 months
9 qualification

7 Test task

1 progress
'Whatever your role, your pay range will be extremely competitive and <u>reviewed in the light of your progress</u>.'

2 five years
'We offer a non-contributory final salary pension scheme, payable from the age of 60 to most <u>staff who have completed the qualifying period of five years</u>.'

3 (residential) clubs
'<u>The business owns a number of residential clubs which offer subsidised holiday accommodation for staff</u> with at least three years' service.'

4 concerts
'<u>Ticket subsidies of 50% of the cost of plays or concerts</u> are available.'

5 leisure skills
'We give generous <u>financial support</u> to staff who wish <u>to acquire leisure skills</u> or continue their education.'

6 loan
'<u>In cases of particular hardship, we will help staff with a loan</u>.'

Reading Worksheet 4

1a Quiz

1 B
The text says, 'We know an adult brain weighs about <u>1.3 kilograms</u>'.

2 B
The text says, 'it's <u>pink</u> and wrinkly'.

3 A
The text says, 'We also know the brain is made up of about <u>100 billion</u> nerve cells'.

4 A
The text says, 'The accident had destroyed his <u>frontal lobe</u>, the part of the brain involved in <u>decision making</u>, social behaviour and impulse control.'

5 B

The text says, 'the brain could not send this information to the language areas on the left side of the brain where it's interpreted'.

6 B

The text says, 'During Brain Awareness Week, it might be a good time to stop and think about your brain, if you rarely do. The week, celebrated annually in March, is an international campaign started in 1995 to raise awareness of the progress and benefits of brain research.'

7 B

The text says, 'The week, celebrated annually in March, is an international campaign started in 1995'.

2

1   Which organ of the body commands more of people's attention than the brain, according to the passage? [a noun]

2   What can the texture of the brain be compared to? [a noun]

3   What place does the arrangement of neurons in the brain resemble? [a noun]

4   Which object penetrated Gage's face, resulting in injury? [a noun]

Get it right!

1   d

2   a

3   b

4   c

1   [your] heart

The text says, 'You run too fast for the bus, and your heart is pounding – telling you to slow down and wait for the next one'.

2   [a] mushroom

The text says, 'it's wrinkly and pink and feels a bit like a mushroom'.

3   [a] telephone exchange

The text says, 'We also know the brain is made up of about 100 billion nerve cells, called "neurons", connected like wires in a telephone exchange.'.

4   [a] metal rod

The text says, 'Some 150 years ago, he was using a metal rod to pack gunpowder into a hole in the rock he was excavating.'

5   rudeness and irresponsibility

The text says, 'Instead of the quiet, unassuming individual he had been before, his behaviour was characterised by rudeness and irresponsibility.'

6   [their] vision

The text says, 'For example, some people suddenly lose the ability to read, even though their vision remains

functioning. They can even write normally, but bizarrely cannot read the words they have just written. This is a condition, known as "alexia without agraphia".'

7   dementia

The text says, 'However, we have barely had an impact on dementia, a brain disease where neurons just wither away and die.'

8   [Roald] Dahl

The text says, 'Another writer, Roald Dahl was fascinated by the impact of disease on the brain. He had the unique claim of helping neurosurgeon Kenneth Till and hydraulic engineer Stanley Wade develop a device known as the "Wade-Dahl-Till" or WDT.'

9   [it] kept jamming

The text says, 'The youngster had previously been fitted with a device called a "Pudenz", but it kept jamming.'

3   Test task

1   [the] [only] rich

The text says, 'The colour purple, for example, extracted from a snail was once so costly that in society at the time only the rich could afford it.'

2   commercial [possibilities]

The text says, 'But perhaps the most fascinating of all Perkin's reactions to his find was his nearly instant recognition that the new dye had commercial possibilities.'

3   [was] [is] mauve

The text says, 'Perkin originally named his dye Tyrian Purple, but it later became commonly known as mauve – from the French from the plant used to make the colour violet.'

4   [Robert] Pullar

The text says, 'He asked the advice of Scottish dye works owner Robert Pullar, who assured him that manufacturing the dye would be well worth it if the colour remained fast'.

5   [in] France

The text says, 'The company received a commercial boost from the Empress Eugenie of France, when she decided the new colour flattered her. Very soon, mauve was the necessary shade for all the fashionable ladies in that country.'

6   [is] malaria

The text says, 'And, in what would have been particularly pleasing to Perkin, their current use is in the search for a vaccine against malaria'.

Writing Worksheet 1

1

A   2

B   4

C   3

Picture 1 is not needed – the camera referred to in extract A was intact and undamaged.

2

A

3

1 B
2 B
3 A
4 B
5 A
6 B

4

1 YES

2 NO – more formal words include 'received' instead of 'got' A; 'extremely' instead of 'very', 'overlooked' instead of 'looked over' and 'stated' instead of 'said' in B; 'additional' instead of 'extra' in C.

3 YES – 'the crockery items were broken' in C.

4 NO – full forms are used throughout the texts: 'I am writing' and 'I had ordered' in A; 'I had been promised' in B; 'I would … like' in C.

5

the problem with the accommodation
what happened when you contacted hotel reception staff
what you would like the manager to do

6

Students' own answers

7a

The first prompt – the student is describing the problem with the accommodation.

7b

I was promised a hotel in a central location, whereas in fact the hotel was located a long distance from the city centre. And to make matters worse, the central heating did not work and so the room was very cold – particularly at night. I had been looking forward to this holiday very much, but it was completely ruined by these issues.

Get it right!

1 I am writing to complain about my recent stay in your hotel.

2 I had been promised a room with a view of the river.

3 I had been looking forward to this holiday very much.

4 My holiday was completely ruined by these issues.

5 I would be grateful if you could refund half the cost of my holiday.

8

Suggested answer

Dear Sir,

I am writing to complain about a recent holiday I booked through CitiDreamz.

First of all, I had been promised a room with a river view, whereas, in fact, my window overlooked a tall block of flats, which made the room extremely dark. Furthermore, the central heating did not work and so the room was very cold – particularly at night. To make matters worse, I had no tea-making facilities in the room, although the website had clearly stated that these would be provided. I had been looking forward to this holiday very much, but it was completely ruined by these issues.

I contacted reception staff to request a change of room and was offered alternative accommodation which was smaller and located directly next to a noisy lift. I had no choice therefore but to remain in the original room I had been allocated for the duration of my stay.

I would therefore be grateful if you could refund half the cost of my holiday in compensation for the considerable disappointment I have experienced.

Yours faithfully,

Ursula Sang

9   Test task

Suggested answer

Dear Sir,

I am writing to complain about an electric travel kettle which I ordered from your store.

First of all, the item arrived one week later than I had expected and the box was also extremely badly damaged. Furthermore, on opening the package I discovered that the kettle was blue rather than the red one I had ordered. And to make matters worse, the lid was cracked and so could not be used. I had been planning to take this kettle on holiday and had placed the order specifically for this purpose.

I tried several times to phone your store to request an immediate replacement, but the phone went unanswered each time. This proved to be not only both extremely time consuming and inconvenient but also added to my frustration.

I would therefore be grateful if you could reimburse the full amount already paid and send me a replacement red kettle free of charge in compensation for the considerable disappointment I have experienced.

Yours faithfully,

Mia Chan

Writing Worksheet 2

1

1 B

2 A

3 C

2

1 C

2 A

3 A

4 B, C

5 A

3

1 formal

say which job you would like to do

explain why you would be suitable for the job

offer availability for one or both months

4

1 B, 2 A, 3 B, 4 B, 5 A

5a

1 waiter

2 the second part – they explain how suitable they are for the job of waiter.

5b

spelling: describe, satisfaction, familiar

verb forms: <u>work</u> well, <u>is</u> extremely important, before I <u>take</u> orders

prepositions: <u>in</u> a hotel, <u>on</u> the menu

capital letters: <u>I</u> understand

I would <u>describe</u> myself as friendly and hard-working. I also <u>work</u> well as part of a team. <u>I</u> understand that <u>in</u> a hotel, customer <u>satisfaction is</u> extremely important so I know I need to be <u>familiar</u> with all the all dishes <u>on</u> the menu before I <u>take</u> orders for lunch or dinner.

6

Suggested answer

Dear Sir or Madam,

I am writing to apply for the job of waiter in your hotel. I am very interested in this position as I am currently doing a hotel management course. I have been fortunate enough to have already gained some valuable experience both in the kitchen and on the front desk of a large hotel in the city. I would therefore like to broaden my experience by learning how to serve customers in a restaurant.

I would describe myself as friendly and hard-working and I work well as part of a team. I also speak several languages so would be able to assist non-English speaking guests by providing translations for particular dishes on the menu.

I am available to work during both July and August because my course does not resume until the beginning of September. I would be grateful if you would consider me for a position of waiter in your hotel. I look forward to hearing from you soon.

Yours faithfully

Orsolya Szabo

7 Test task

Suggested answer

Dear Sir or Madam,

I am writing to apply for the job of instructor on the children's activity camp. I am particularly interested in this position as I am currently doing a sports management course at university. I have been fortunate enough to have already gained some valuable experience as a volunteer coach, teaching adults in a local football club. I would therefore like to broaden my experience by teaching sports to children.

I am an experienced footballer and tennis player and so would be confident in teaching both these sporting activities. I am currently goalkeeper for my university football team and have been playing tennis for many years. I have taken part in tournaments at local as well as national level and have won several trophies, including gold and silver.

I am available to work throughout the summer holidays as my course does not resume until early autumn. I would therefore be very grateful if you could consider me for the position and look forward to hearing from you soon.

Yours faithfully

Sarah Mark

Writing Worksheet 3

1b

informal

2

1 A

2 B

3 A

4 A, B

5 B

6 B

7 B

3

A

> Great news! I'm writing to let you know that at last we've moved house! <u>We just couldn't go on</u> living in the two-bedroom flat now that the twins are growing up and the new baby has arrived. <u>We've got</u> three bedrooms now, and <u>there's</u> a very modern bathroom and a spacious kitchen too. So, <u>would you like to</u> come round for dinner on Saturday evening – say 7pm? Let me know if that's good for you. Can't wait to find out what you think of our new place!

— EXPLAINING
— DESCRIBING
— INVITING

B

> <u>I'm really sorry but</u> I won't be able to pick you up from the station on Friday. My car broke down yesterday and <u>I've had to take it to the garage for repair and it won't be ready for me to collect until next week</u>. I'm not at all happy that it's going to take as long as that to get fixed. <u>What a pain!</u> So <u>it'd be best</u> to take the number 43 bus into the city centre. I'll meet you there instead. Then, <u>how about</u> we find a nice café where we can sit down and have something to eat? Let me know what you think.

— APOLOGISING
— EXPLAINING
— COMPLAINING
— ADVISING
— SUGGESTING

4

1 YES (both texts are friendly in tone)

2 YES (Both Texts have exclamation marks. Text A: 'Great news!' and 'I'm writing to let you know that at last we've moved house!' Text B: 'What a pain!')

3 NO (Neither text uses full forms – there are contractions throughout both texts)

4 YES (Both texts have incomplete sentences. Text A: 'Great news!' and Text B: 'What a pain!')

5 YES (Both texts have phrasal verbs. Text A: 'go on' meaning continue, 'growing up' and 'come round' meaning visit; Text B: 'pick you up' meaning collect and 'sit down')

5a

explain why you have moved

describe the new city

invite your friend to come and visit

5b

Students' own ideas

6a

The student is writing about the second prompt – describing the new city.

6b

The student uses full forms instead of contractions. He follows all the other advice given in the checklist.

(He includes an exclamation mark 'Great fun!'

He includes phrasal verbs: 'come across' meaning discover, 'look out over' meaning overlooks.)

6c

Leeds really is a lively city. <u>You'd</u> love it here! <u>It's</u> a university city so there are lots of young people around. <u>There's</u> always something new and exciting to do. Great fun! <u>I've</u> come across some amazing music venues where there are some live bands at weekends. My flat looks out over a lovely park and <u>it's</u> a great place to go jogging or have a picnic – especially when the <u>weather's</u> good.

7

Suggested answer

Dear Beata

I'm writing to let you know that I've moved to Leeds! You'll remember that I told you that I'd applied for a job as a manager of a garden centre – well, I got it! I'm really enjoying the work. I've got some really nice colleagues and the customers are friendly too.

Leeds really is a lively city. You'd love it here! It's a university city so there are lots of young people around. There's always something new and exciting to do. Great fun! I've already come across some amazing music venues where there are some live bands at weekends. My new flat looks out over a lovely park and it's a great place to go jogging or have a picnic – especially when the weather's good.

So how about coming here for a visit one weekend? I could meet you at the station and show you all the sights and my new place, of course. You've got my phone number so give me a call and we can fix a date.

See you soon,

Anya

8 Test task

Suggested answer

Dear Dave

I'm writing to let you know that at last we've moved to a bigger house! We just couldn't go on living in the two-bedroom bungalow now that the twins are growing up and the new baby's arrived. So, we started looking

– and one thing led to another and we're now settled in our new home!

I'm sure you'll like it as much as us. We've got three bedrooms now, and there's a very modern bathroom and kitchen too. The kids are happy because they've got so much more space now with the big living room and the garden outside. But Michael's the happiest of all because there's hardly any decorating to do!

Why don't you come round this weekend and see what you think of our new place? We'd love to see you and if the weather's nice we can all have a barbecue in the garden.

Our new address and phone number are below, so give us a call and let us know what time you'll be here.

Best wishes

Francine

Writing Worksheet 4

1a

1 Picture B   2 Picture C   3 Picture A

1b

a exhibits   b interactive   c souvenir   d collection
e jewellery   f on display   g accessible   h life-size
i sculpture   j preserving

2b

B

3

Students' own notes

4b

View 1: 1, 3, 5   View 2: 2, 4

5

4:   Some people think that

6

Students' own notes

7

1 E   2 D   3 B   4 C   5 A

8b

1   The writer supports the first view – the view that admission charges are fair and reasonable.

2   The writer mentions Statement 1 in Exercise 4a about museums being expensive to run and also Statement 5 about people having to pay for other leisure activities.

3   Yes, in Paragraph 2. The writer makes reference to Statement 4 in Exercise 4a that admission charges could deter poorer people from going to museums.

4   Yes, the writer mentions that museums are free of charge on Mondays in their home city.

8c

1 D   2 B   3 A   4 C

9

Students' own paragraphs

10b

A

11

Students' own paragraphs

12   Test task

Suggested answer

Many schools organise trips and excursions to a variety of cultural institutions, including art galleries, natural history and science museums, as well as theatres, wildlife parks and historical sites. Some people take the view that these kinds of visits can enhance learning, while others think that a student's time is best spent within a classroom setting. I firmly believe that these visits should be compulsory.

Some people argue that trips and excursions may distract students from their coursework and their progress towards examinations. However, many museums provide events that are relevant to subjects taught in school. For example, in my city, there is an annual Science Festival which includes interactive workshops on many of the topics covered in subjects like Physics.

However, there is no doubt that students can learn a great deal by learning outside the confines of the classroom. A visit to a Science Festival event can enable students to interact with a variety of different exhibits – such as a wave machine. These can help bring the subject to life and enable students to 'learn by doing'. Furthermore, they can contribute to the development of students into mature adults with the critical thinking and problem-solving skills they will need in their future lives. Finally, it is impossible to argue against the fact that learning is about more than examination success. Surely schools have a responsibility to promote a love of learning for its own sake. For example, a visit to a concert might encourage a lifelong passion for classical music.

All in all, I strongly believe that these kinds of trips should form an integral part of high school programmes. Schools have a responsibility to ensure that students have exposure to the world around them and what better way to do this than to step outside the classroom.

Writing Worksheet 5

1

You are being asked to say whether you agree or disagree with governments imposing a higher tax on short domestic flights.

2

1 domestic tourism   2 green energy

3 sustainable travel   4 air pollution   5 eco-friendly

6 diesel fuel   7 global warming

8 offsetting your emissions   9 large carbon footprint

3

Good for the environment: domestic tourism, eco-friendly, green energy, offsetting your emissions, sustainable travel

Bad for environment: air pollution, diesel fuel, global warming, large carbon footprint

4b

C (I firmly believe that tackling the problem of global warming needs far more than a simple tax to make people reconsider how they travel.)

5

1 A / agree   2 D / disagree   3 A / agree

4 A / agree   5 D/ disagree

6

1 C   2 E   3 A   4 D   5 B

7

1 despite   2 although, despite   3 but

4 Nevertheless, However

Get it right!

1   <u>Although</u> fewer flights would mean more trains, this could place pressure on the rail network.

2   Travelling by rail or bus may take longer than flying, <u>but</u> you get to see more of the country than you would by sitting on a plane.

8

Students' own answers

9a

Main idea: People living in remote areas don't have a choice of travel.

9b

despite   Although   but   Nevertheless

10

Students' own answers

11

Governments could encourage airlines to design planes

that use greener fuels.

Invest more in bus and rail services

Educate people about sustainable travel

12

Suggested answer

There is no doubt that an increasing number of people are choosing to take domestic flights these days and this is having a serious impact on the environment. This is because these individual short trips can have a remarkably large carbon footprint. However, despite the high CO2 emissions emitted, I strongly believe that tackling the problem of climate change is likely to need more than a simple tax.

Although there can be no doubt that short flights are responsible for a lot of carbon emissions, imposing a tax is unlikely to discourage people from flying short distances – particularly those who live in remote areas and have no other option but to fly. Furthermore, it is sometimes the case that it is cheaper for travellers to fly than to take the train or the car.

Nevertheless, there are various other measures that could help to reduce greenhouse gas emissions. Firstly, governments could persuade airlines to design planes which have more efficient engines and use cleaner fuels. Furthermore, there needs to be more investment in improving bus and rail services and ensuring that these run efficiently. Finally, I think that there is a need for more education about the effects of global warming and how cutting back on air travel could have a positive impact. Some people simply do not realise just how polluting short flights are.

In conclusion, I think that imposing a tax on domestic flights would have a limited impact on addressing the serious issue of climate change. It is far more useful to educate the public about the importance of sustainable travel and for governments to construct and run efficient rail and bus systems.

13   Test task

Suggested answer

There is no doubt that traffic and pollution from vehicles have become huge problems, both in cities and on motorways everywhere. Solving these problems is likely to need more than a simple rise in the price of petrol.

Although private car use is one of the main causes of the increase in traffic and pollution, higher fuel costs are unlikely to limit the number of drivers for long. Increasing the price of fuel may also have an impact on the cost of public transport – bus companies would likely expect customers to pay higher fares to help fund the extra fuel costs. This would be extremely unpopular with everyone who needs to travel on the roads. But there are various other measures that could be implemented that would have a huge effect on these problems.

In my opinion, to tackle the problem of pollution, cleaner fuels need to be developed. The technology is already available to produce electric cars that would be both quieter and cleaner to use. Persuading manufacturers and travellers to adopt this new technology would be a more effective strategy for improving air quality, especially in cities.

However, traffic congestion will not be solved by changing the type of private vehicle people can use. To do this, we need to improve the choice of public transport services available to travellers. For example, if more bus stations and underground train systems were built and effectively maintained in our major cities, then traffic on the roads would be dramatically reduced.

In conclusion, I think that long-term traffic and pollution reductions would depend on promoting the use of cleaner technology and on government using public money to construct and run efficient public transport systems.

Speaking Worksheet 1

1

1 alike   2 like   3 like doing   4 look like / like

NARRATOR: Track 31
Speaking Worksheet 1

EXAMINER: Are you and your friends alike?

What are your family like?

What do you and your friends like doing together?

Who, in your family, do you look like most?

2

1 D   2 B   3 A   4 C

NARRATOR: Track 32
Speaking Worksheet 1

NARRATOR: 1

EXAMINER: Are you and your friends alike?

STUDENT: I'm like my best friend Martha. We're both quite impatient and when it comes to sports, we're very competitive as we hate losing.

NARRATOR: 2

EXAMINER: What are your family like?

STUDENT: Well, mum's tall and elegant and, um, quite strict – especially about things like keeping my room tidy, or when I want to stay out late with my mates.

NARRATOR: 3

EXAMINER: What do you and your friends like doing together?

STUDENT: A It depends on the weather really. If it's nice, we love chilling out in the park. It helps us relax after a hard day at college.

NARRATOR: 4

EXAMINER: Who, in your family, do you look like most?

STUDENT: That'll be my dad. Our features are very similar; for example, we've got the same chin and nose.

3

1   X In English, it is generally considered rude to say 'What?' if you do not hear what someone has said to you.

2   OK In English, 'Pardon?' means that you did not hear what someone has said to you.

3   OK In English, 'Sorry' has several meanings. One meaning is that you did not hear what someone has said to you.

4   X It is not natural to say 'Repeat?' if you do not hear what someone has said to you. If you want to use 'repeat', you should use it in a phrase, for example, 'Could you repeat that please?'

4

2   Could you repeat the question?

3   Would you mind saying that again please?

NARRATOR: Track 33
Speaking Worksheet 1

STUDENT: I didn't quite catch that. Could you say it again please?

Sorry, I missed that. Could you repeat the question?

I couldn't quite hear you. Would you mind saying that again please?

5

1 B   2 A   3 D   4 C

NARRATOR: Track 34
Speaking Worksheet 1

NARRATOR: A

EXAMINER: What do you like about your home town or city?

STUDENT:	Well, there's a lot to do which is great. My best friend and I often go to the cinema. Last week we saw a 3D film. It was amazing. The special effects were super cool and the acting superb. My favourite genre of film is horror. I just love it, you know, when a film makes me jump out of my seat in fear.
NARRATOR:	B
EXAMINER:	Do you think your hometown has changed much in recent years?
STUDENT:	Not really, no.
EXAMINER:	Why not?
STUDENT:	I dunno.
NARRATOR:	C
EXAMINER:	Is your hometown a popular place for tourists to visit?
STUDENT:	Yes, it's a popular holiday destination. Mainly due to our amazing sandy beach and then there are great cultural attractions, like the castle ruins and the museum.
NARRATOR:	D
EXAMINER:	Do you prefer the summer or winter in your hometown?
STUDENT:	That's an interesting question. I was talking to my friend about this last week. While some would argue that summer is the best time of year, in my opinion, I prefer winter.

6

Words and phrases to give examples	Words and phrases to give reasons
for instance	as
like	due to
including	since
such as	this happens because

7

1 B 2 E 3 C 4 G 5 A 6 D 7 F

8 Test task

Example notes:

1 like football / as I get to keep fit / spend time with mates

2 football as footballing nation / cycling for instance / due to success in the Tour de France

Laya didn't say what she would personally like to try, but instead talks about what's popular in her country.

3 Occasionally, if it was an important international match, like the World Cup / always preferred to go outside

4 Laya uses the phrase, 'I didn't quite catch that' to let the examiner know she didn't hear the question clearly.

football at primary school / … including tennis and basketball at senior school / almost all senior schools have a basketball team, for example

NARRATOR:	🔊 Track 35 Speaking Worksheet 1
EXAMINER:	Let's talk about sports. Do you enjoy playing sports?
LAYA:	Yes, I do. I particularly like taking part in team sports, like football, as I get to keep fit and also spend time with my mates.
EXAMINER:	Is there any sport you would you like to try in the future?
LAYA:	Well, I'd have to say football is the most popular sport as we're a footballing nation, although more recently other sports, um, cycling for instance, have become really popular. Cycling is due to our success in the Tour de France, I expect.
EXAMINER:	Do you often watch sport on TV?
LAYA:	No, I didn't, not really. I mean, occasionally, if it was an important international football match, like the World Cup um since I love football … but to be honest, I've always preferred to go outside and play football rather than watching it indoors.
EXAMINER:	What sports do children normally do at school in your country?
LAYA:	Sorry, I didn't quite catch that. Did you say 'at school'?
EXAMINER:	Yes, that's right.
LAYA:	Hm well, when I was at school, there was football of course and children of all ages get taught that – even in primary school. Then, at senior school, kids can play other sports including tennis and basketball. I think almost all senior schools have a basketball team, for example.
EXAMINER:	Thank you.

9

Students' own answers

Speaking Worksheet 2

1

See underlining in Track 36.

1 A   2 B   3 B   4 A   5 B

NARRATOR: 🔊 **Track 36**
Speaking Worksheet 2

CHANGYING: Hey Abbas. How's it going?

ABBAS: Hello Changying. I'm good. Just trying to revise for my IELTS Speaking test next week.

CHANGYING: I'm struggling with my revision.

ABBAS: Why?

CHANGYING: Well, it's Part Two that's keeping me awake at night.

ABBAS: Ah you're worried because you're not sure what to say for two minutes?

CHANGYING: Well, there is that though it's more about speaking alone, <u>specifically without any questions from the examiner.</u>

ABBAS: I know what you mean; however, there's a task card isn't there, plus what's really useful is you get a minute to prepare what you want to talk about.

CHANGYING: I guess.

ABBAS: What revision strategies are you using?

CHANGYING: Right well, <u>I think it's good to memorise answers – that way you can use the same vocabulary and phrases no matter what.</u>

ABBAS: <u>I'm not sure that's an effective use of revision time.</u> It's unlikely you'll get the same topic in the real test and you'll just sound unnatural. I think knowing how to correctly talk about the past, present and future, as well as being fluent, is the best option.

CHANGYING: Ah you might be right.

ABBAS: What about pronunciation?

CHANGYING: Hmm I guess I could improve that by <u>recording and listening to myself which I reckon is better than listening to local people.</u>

ABBAS: I also think it is a good idea to time yourself answering a Part Two question.

CHANGYING: Why's that?

ABBAS: Well, <u>so you get to know what speaking for one to two minutes feels like.</u> When you're answering the question in the test, you'll probably be too nervous to think about that.

CHANGYING: I agree. Is it OK to tell a lie – you know make something up?

ABBAS: Well, you won't lose marks, but if you ask me, the best answers are about real personal experiences.

CHANGYING: You're right. That way I might feel a bit more confident about <u>expanding on my ideas, you know, by giving examples for instance.</u>

ABBAS: Don't forget if you talk about something that's happened, or will happen; then you'll sound more natural too.

2

See underlining in Track 37.

1 wanted me to talk about   2 with that in mind
3 the sort of people who typically   4 Regarding its
5 about the reason

NARRATOR: 🔊 **Track 37**
Speaking Worksheet 2

CHANGYING: <u>You wanted me to talk about a local shop I go to every so often. So, with that in mind,</u> I'm going to talk about a shop called New From Old which sells furniture like coffee tables, chairs and lamp shades. I think the <u>sort of people who typically go there are</u> people **like my Aunt Miriam, for example**. She's a designer. Actually, she designs and makes cushions from old sheets and jumpers which she sells in New From Old. Anyway, **it's people like her who tend to go there** because the stuff they sell is so unique and I think designers and, you know, creative people like that. <u>Regarding its location, it's not far from where I live</u> in the old part of the city.

When I say not far, **I mean** I can walk there from home in around twenty minutes.

There are a lot of, well, arty shops in the same street. You know, erm, such as shops that sell artisan bread, hand-made jewellery … So, it's located in a good spot, I think. What about the reason why I like shopping in New From Old? Well, **as I said**, Aunt Miriam's cushions are sold there, **but it's more than that**. New From Old is all about recycling and reusing, for example, they take things that people are going to throw away, like an old table and they give it new life. You know, **they repair it**, paint it vibrant colours and then sell it to someone who does want it. I bought a lamp from them last week and it was made from old tyres which were painted white. I mean amazing, right?

So that's why I go there really – it takes things that no one wants anymore and turns them into something special and as I don't agree with waste – well, I think it's a super idea for a shop.

3

See **bold** text in Track 37.

1 C   2 A   3 H   4 G   5 B   6 F   7 E

D is not needed.

4

When writing notes, do not try and write down everything you want to say. Instead think about a few detailed phrases and ideas that you can expand on when you are speaking. Whatever note-taking style you use, your notes should be clear enough to follow. Remember, IELTS Part 2 is not a test of knowledge but a test of how you communicate about a topic, so use the one minute you have before you start speaking to write notes effectively.

5

Example notes:

What: Sports car / Porsche 918 718 Boxster to be precise

How long: early teens / around 10 years ago

Where: Not (entirely) sure / out walking with dad / local park / used to be a football coach

Why: You might think looks: low & sleek / however: deep sound / performance: premium car / I'll be a proud owner

---

NARRATOR: 🔊 Track 38
Speaking Worksheet 2

ABBAS: Right, well the thing I really would like to have that I don't already is a sports car. A Porsche 718 Boxster, to be precise. I reckon the first time I saw one, I was in my early teens, about thirteen or fourteen years old, so around ten years ago now. As for where? Well, to be honest, I'm not entirely sure – I was out walking with my dad, so I think it was near the local park. Yeah, that's right, we were on our way back from playing football – my dad used to be the team coach – and it just went past us.

You might think it's the way it looks, you know, low, two-seater, sleek; however, actually, it's the sound it makes. That sort of deep rumble. I just love it. Then of course, it's the performance. I've read about it since, and the Boxster is a premium car. At least that's what I think and that's the reason why one day, once I've saved and saved, I'll be the proud owner of one.

---

6   Test task

Students' own answers

Speaking Worksheet 3

1

A   Which skills should children learn at school? / At school, which skills should children learn? / Children should learn which skills at school?

B   Are there any skills which they should learn at home?

C   Which skills and abilities will be important in the future? / Which abilities and skills will be important in the future? / In the future which skills and abilities will be important? / In the future which abilities and skills will be important?

2

See underlining in Track 39.

Techniques for developing ideas:	✓ / ✗	Explanation
1 giving your own point of view or opinion	✓	'seems to me' and 'Personally': the speaker is providing their own opinion.
2 giving others' points of view or ideas	✓	'some might say': the speaker is providing hypothetical opinions of unnamed people.
3 suggesting a solution to a problem	✓	'one way of dealing with this': the speaker has provided a problem and has suggested one solution is to 'teach life skills'.
4 explaining why something happens	✓	'Because of this' and 'instance': the speaker provides two explanations.
5 offering a contrasting idea	✗	The speaker doesn't provide any contrasting ideas.
6 making future predictions	✓	'likely to need': the speaker is predicting that we're 'likely to need' technology skills to deal with a changing world.
7 explaining advantages and/or disadvantages of something	✓	'Technology offers us, and the planet, huge potential benefits': the Speaker says that technology is a 'huge' 'benefit', meaning an advantage. However, the word 'potential' can imply that there could be disadvantages (these are not named or further explained).
8 giving examples to support ideas	✓	'as an example': the Speaker provides an example of socialising to support the argument.
9 giving factual information	✗	The Speaker provides no quoted, factual information. Everything mentioned is based on personal opinion and hypothetical ideas.

NARRATOR: 🔊 **Track 39**
Speaking Worksheet 3

EXAMINER: We've been talking about skills and abilities, and I'd like to ask you a few more questions. So, first of all, which skills do you think children should learn at school?

BERDINE: Well, it <u>seems to me</u> that children don't behave as well as they used to, and one way <u>of dealing with</u> this is to teach life skills. Let's take socialising <u>as an example</u>. Children these days spend too much time in front of computers. <u>Because of this</u>, they don't know how to properly form relationships face to face – socialise with their peers, communicate – things like that. So, I think schools ought to pick it up.

EXAMINER: Right, thank you. So, are there any skills which children should learn at home?

BERDINE: Hm, well <u>some might say</u> that life skills, or specifically the social skills I mentioned before, ought to be taught at home, but that's not always possible for one reason or another. Um for <u>instance</u>, they may have no siblings or even friends nearby to play with. <u>Personally</u>, I think children should learn from their parents how to love and respect themselves and others. That's really important, you know, for a child's future.

EXAMINER: I see, and which skills and abilities will be important in the future?

BERDINE: Hm, let me think. Right well, technology is advancing all the time, isn't it? The world is really changing. So, I think we're <u>likely to need</u> skills related to that. So, IT programming and computer design and creativity and well, we need to be able to solve complex problems, things like that, to tackle issues like global warming. <u>Technology offers us, and the planet, huge potential benefits</u>, so developing any skills and abilities related to that will be the most important.

3

See underlining in Track 39.

1 seems to me   2 of dealing with   3 as an example.

4 Because of this   5 some might say   6 instance
7 Personally   8 likely to need   9 huge potential benefits

4

1 giving others' points of view or ideas
2 discussing advantages and/or disadvantages of something
3 giving examples to support ideas
4 suggesting a solution to a problem
5 giving your own point of view or opinion
6 making future predictions
7 offering a contrasting idea
8 giving factual information
9 explaining why something happens

5

Disagree	Neither disagree nor agree	Agree
I'm not so sure about that.	That depends on the situation.	My thoughts exactly.
That's not the way I see it.	I think we need to consider both sides.	There's no doubt about it.

6

1 Advik neither agrees nor disagrees with the opinion.
2 Advik uses the phrase, 'I'm in two minds' to express his view.
3 In agreement: Advik develops his ideas by using the example of a footballer's salary and a doctor's salary and says it would be 'fairer' if they were paid the same: 'doctors save lives … if someone needs major heart surgery'.

    In disagreement: Advik uses a firefighter and aircraft pilot as examples of jobs which people might not want to do if all salaries were equal.

NARRATOR: **Track 40**
Speaking Worksheet 3

EXAMINER: Some people say it would be better for society if everyone got the same salary. What do you think about that?

ADVIK: Well, to be honest, I'm in two minds about that really. I can see if we were to all get paid the same, then things might feel fairer; take a footballer's salary compared to a doctor's, for example. I mean, footballers get paid vast amounts of money to kick a ball whereas doctors get paid a lot less to save lives … You know, if someone needs major heart surgery,

---

something like that. On the other hand, if all salaries were equal, then people might not want to do challenging or high-risk jobs like becoming a firefighter or aircraft pilot.

---

7   Test task

Students' own answers

Get it right!

RAJ:

Well, I don't believe that having a lot of possessions will necessarily equal success in the future. For me, being successful will be about having a happy and healthy family rather than the number of items I own.

This is not the best candidate response. Although the candidate talks about whether owning possessions in the future will be a sign of success and gives a supporting example, their answer is personal and does not discuss the views of other people generally.

MARIA:

Not really, no. I think the focus on having good mental health will continue and for many, success will be more about living a stress-free life, for example, less work and more family time, than buying flash cars.

This is the best candidate response. The candidate discusses a possible view of other people and speaks generally, 'the focus on having good mental health will … *for many* (for many people)'. A supporting example is given.

HANU:

Absolutely. My dad really wants to own a premium car, like a Lamborghini, in the future. He thinks it will show other people how successful he is. I'd like lots of expensive possessions in the future too.

This is not the best answer. Although the candidate talks about the future and the connection between owning possessions and success, the candidate uses a personal example, (dad), and does not discuss the views of other people generally.

Think about it

Listening Worksheet 1

1 in the order you hear them
2 don't choose
3 Word matching
4 the same idea / a different way
5 will
6 Only one
7 once
8 speaker

Listening Worksheet 2

1 TRUE
2 TRUE
3 FALSE
4 FALSE (always follow not sometimes)
5 TRUE
6 FALSE Keep listening and continue to the next question.
7 FALSE There will always be options you do not need.
8 TRUE

Listening Worksheet 3

1 h
2 d
3 b
4 g
5 c
6 a
7 e
8 f

Listening Worksheet 4

1 monologue
2 directions
3 location
4 tourist
5 question
6 letters
7 compass
8 orientate

Listening Worksheet 5

1 TRUE
2 FALSE Your answer will be marked wrong.
3 FALSE Your answer will be marked wrong.
4 TRUE
5 FALSE They may appear in any part of the test.
6 FALSE You will be asked to complete a gap.
7 TRUE
8 TRUE

Listening Worksheet 6

1 might hear
2 correct answer
3 unanswered
4 Guess
5 specific
6 the exact
7 Use
8 follow

Reading Worksheet 1

1 statements
2 place
3 paraphrases
4 questions
5 text
6 jump
7 key
8 beginning

Reading Worksheet 2

1 TRUE
2 FALSE They often contain the same words.
3 TRUE
4 FALSE They are in the order of the text.
5 TRUE
6 FALSE The answer is NOT GIVEN; if the answer is FALSE, the text will give the opposite information.
7 TRUE
8 TRUE

Reading Worksheet 3

1 b
2 h
3 g
4 a
5 d
6 e
7 c
8 f

Reading Worksheet 4

1 will
2 words
3 is
4 should not
5 correct
6 will
7 question word
8 incorrect

Writing Worksheet 1

1 FALSE It should be formal.
2 TRUE
3 FALSE Contractions are informal.
4 TRUE
5 TRUE
6 FALSE Keep to the word limit.
7 FALSE Write about all three bullet points.
8 TRUE

Writing Worksheet 2

1 formal
2 all
3 proofread
4 Yours faithfully
5 Don't include
6 150
7 Please will you
8 can

Writing Worksheet 3

1 informal
2 friendly
3 exclamations
4 full
5 manager
6 formal
7 functions
8 description

Writing Worksheet 4

1 FALSE You must answer both questions.
2 TRUE
3 FALSE Use a formal and academic style.
4 FALSE Write a minimum of 250 words.
5 TRUE
6 TRUE
7 FALSE It should include an introduction and a conclusion.
8 TRUE

Writing Worksheet 5

1 two
2 must
3 linking words
4 despite
5 will
6 important
7 do have
8 paragraphs

Speaking Worksheet 1

1 familiar
2 dislikes
3 naturally
4 reasons
5 repeat
6 penalised
7 correct
8 five

Speaking Worksheet 2

1 g
2 a
3 e
4 h
5 c
6 f
7 b
8 d

Speaking Worksheet 3

1 FALSE You can agree, disagree or partially agree with an opinion given in the question.
2 TRUE
3 FALSE It lasts four to five minutes.
4 FALSE It is important to develop ideas with reasons, examples and solutions.
5 TRUE
6 FALSE It is fine to give factual information.
7 TRUE
8 TRUE

ACKNOWLEDGEMENTS

The authors and publishers acknowledge the following sources of copyright material and are grateful for the permissions granted. While every effort has been made, it has not always been possible to identify the sources of all the material used, or to trace all copyright holders. If any omissions are brought to our notice, we will be happy to include the appropriate acknowledgements on reprinting and in the next update to the digital edition, as applicable.

Key: LWK = Listening Worksheet, RWK = Reading Worksheet, SWK = Speaking Worksheet, WWK = Writing Worksheet

Text

RWK2: Fire and Rescue NSW for the adapted text from 'Smoke alarms in the home'. Copyright © 2021 Fire and Rescue NSW. Reproduced with kind permission; **RWK3:** On the Job for the text adapted from 'Greenkeeper – Environments'. Copyright © On The Job. Reproduced with kind permission; John Lewis Partnership for the adapted text from 'John Lewis Benefits', www.jlpjobs.com. Reproduced with permission. **RWK4:** The Independent for the text adapted from 'The mystery of the incredible human brain' by Tom Solomon. Copyright © Tom Solomon/The Independent. Reproduced with permission.

Photography

The following images have been sourced from Getty Images.

LWK1: Stephen Frink/The Image Bank; **LWK2:** fstop123/E+; franckreporter/E+; Poike/iStock / Getty Images Plus; **LWK3:** guruXOOX/iStock Getty Images Plus; **LWK4:** Artur Debat/Moment; John Lund/Photodisc; Francesco Bergamaschi/Moment; **LWK5:** Image Source; EThamPhoto/The Image Bank; Poshey Aherne / 500px; **RWK1:** gerenme/iStock/Getty Images Plus; **RWK2:** Nazar Abbas Photography/Moment; **RWK3:** gsermek/iStock/Getty Images Plus; **RWK4:** Monty Rakusen/Image Source; Science & Society Picture Librar/SSPL; **WWK1:** DieterMeyrl/iStock / Getty Images Plus; Akintevs/iStock/Getty Images Plus; Sunny/DigitalVision; d3sign/Moment; **WWK2:** Alphotographic/ iStock Unreleased; Maskot; FatCamera/E+; **WWK3:** Bruce Bennett Studios; **WWK4:** Atstock Productions/iStock/Getty Images Plus; Indeed; **WWK5:** guvendemir/iStock/Getty Images Plus; **SWK1:** Jack Hollingsworth; **SWK2:** 10'000 Hours/DigitalVision.

Audio

Audio production by Sounds Like Mike.

Typesetting

Typeset by Blooberry Design.

The publishers would also like to thank the following for their contributions to this project: Trish Chapman, Judith Wilson and Carole Allsop.